THE WHITE HOUSE

★ AN ILLUSTRATED TOUR ★

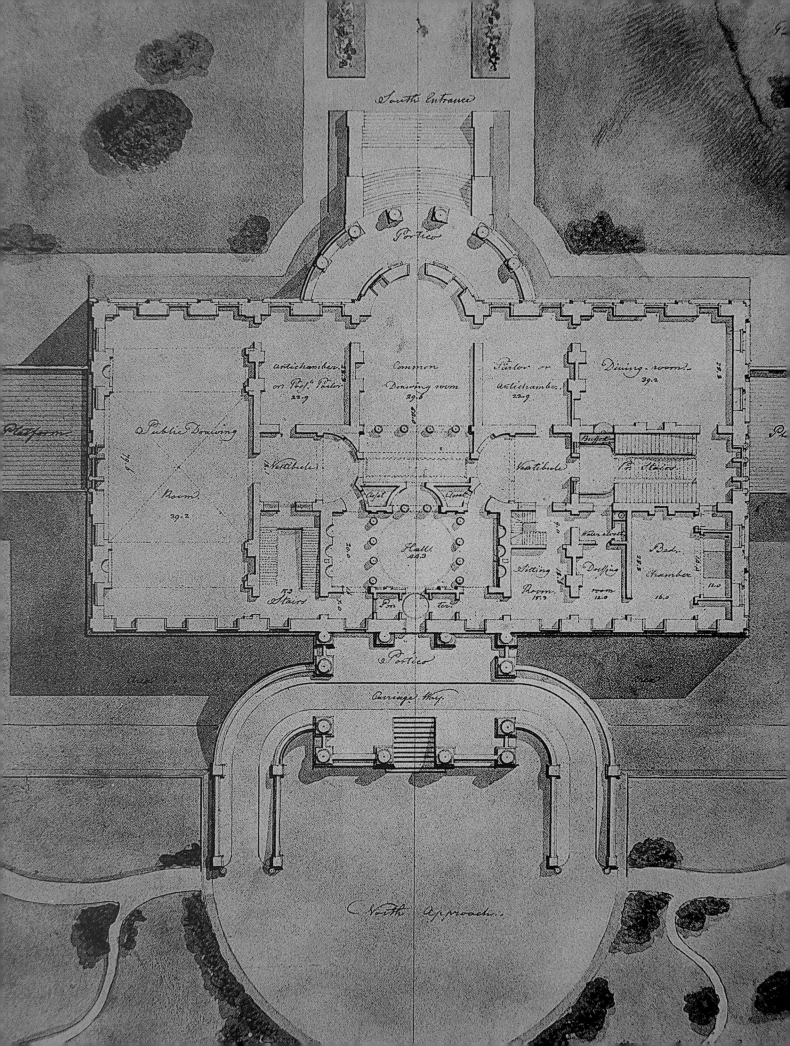

South Entrance

Portico

Platform

Public Drawing

Room.
39.2

Antichamber.
or Best Parlor
22.9

Common
Drawing room
29.6

Parlor or
Antichamber.
22.9

Dining room
39.2

Vestibule

Vestibule

Pr. Stairs

Buffet

Stairs

Closet

Closet

Hall
44.3

Sitting
Room
15.3

Dressing
room
12.0

Water closet

Bed
Chamber
16.0

Porter

Portico

Carriage Way.

North Approach.

THE WHITE HOUSE

★ AN ILLUSTRATED TOUR ★

BY BILL HARRIS

COURAGE
BOOKS

AN IMPRINT OF RUNNING PRESS
PHILADELPHIA • LONDON

THE WHITE HOUSE

CREDITS

Editor: Phil Hunt
Designer: Mark Holt
Commissioning Editor: Will Steeds
Project Manager: Stella Caldwell
Picture Research: Terry Forshaw
Artifact photography: Don Eiler, Richmond, VA
   ©Salamander Books Ltd
Production: Phillip Chamberlain
Color reproduction: Media Print, London, England

This book may be ordered by mail from the
publisher. But try your bookstore first!

Visit us on the web!
www.runningpress.com

Contents

Foreword   6.

Prologue   8.

1 The Background   10

2 The House as a Home   26

3 A New Century   56

4 The Grand Tour   78

Afterword   92

Acknowledgments   96

Foreword

Of all of America's architectural icons, none has quite the same deep intimate meaning as the home of the president—the White House in Washington, D.C. Its address, 1600 Pennsylvania Avenue, is as familiar to most of us as our own home address.

Although the idea of royalty was an anathema to the Founding Fathers, and is still an alien concept to all Americans, we have come to regard the White House as our very own version of a royal palace. Indeed, during the Kennedy administration, it was known as "Camelot," for the royal court of King Arthur. No one regarded the comparison as the least bit strange.

We are fascinated by the pageantry and the ceremony that takes place there. We are eager to know more about the private lives of the people who live there. We see television reporters on its lawn virtually every night. And if we've never actually seen the Rose Garden, we know that we could find our way around it.

By law, the lease anyone can hold on this place can only last a short eight years. But that only adds to its fascination. Every president and his family have put a personal stamp on it. They have redecorated it to suit their own personal style, and they have rebuilt parts of it to protect its place in history. Each and every one of them has left behind stories and legends that year after year have added up to a legacy that makes the White House more than just a building, but a treasured national institution.

The threat of terrorism has put the White House temporarily off-limits to visitors, but it is still very much the People's House, just as it always has been since its first resident, John Adams, graciously welcomed everyone who came to his door.

After more than 200 years, the White House is arguably more beautiful than it has been at any time in its history. It was officially designated a museum in 1988, but it is still very much a home. It is much more than just the home of the incumbent president, it is still what the American people have always been proud to call their own.

The images in the following pages may serve as a substitute for an in-person tour of the White House, but this tribute is much more than that. It is a celebration of all the tradition that this building has represented to every American for more than two centuries.

Prologue

After he retired from the presidency, Benjamin Harrison said that "There has never been an hour since I left the White House that I have felt a wish return to it." William McKinley wasn't interested in renewing the lease, either. "I have had all the honor that there is in this place," he said.

John Adams said, "If I were to go over my life again, I would be a shoemaker." And his son, John Quincy Adams, called his days in the White House, "The four most miserable years of my life."

The day Abraham Lincoln moved in, his predecessor, James Buchanan said, "If you are as happy, my dear sir, on entering the White House as I in leaving it, you are the happiest man in the country." William Howard Taft called it "the lonesomest place in the world." And Warren G. Harding compared it to a prison.

Of course, they were all talking about the job, not the house.

Yet, every four years, two men—and someday maybe a woman or two—square off and fight with all their might for a chance to move into the White House. Former president Grover Cleveland even came out of retirement and moved back into his former home. Theodore Roosevelt tried to do the same thing, but was denied the opportunity.

Naysayers notwithstanding, when all is said and done, there simply isn't a better place to live in all of America than 1600 Pennsylvania Avenue in Washington, D.C.—the place we call the White House.

1 The Background

After he was inaugurated as America's first president in New York City, George Washington lived in a borrowed house that, like the place where he took the oath of office, has long since been demolished. But he knew that the home of the president would be important to the country's perception of the office.

RIGHT

While work went forward on the Federal City and the President's House, President George Washington kept an eye on the progress from his plantation, Mount Vernon, a few miles down the Potomac River.

FAR RIGHT

An 1807 drawing by Benjamin Latrobe shows the first major change in the design of the White House: the addition of the North and South porticos ordered by Thomas Jefferson.

Washington's Virginia plantation covered about 500 acres, tended largely by slaves. After he retired from the presidency, he was forced to sell off some of it to make ends meet. But he managed to live the life of a country gentleman until the day he died, in 1799, of a strep throat, an ailment easily cured today.

Even before he left his plantation at Mount Vernon, Virginia, he told James Madison that, "...it is my wish and intention to conform to the public desire and expectation with respect to the style proper for the Chief Magistrate to live in."

The style was set by a generous congress which appropriated enough money to furnish the new president's temporary digs in a style that can only be described as lavish. There were Turkish carpets on the floors, and fine papers on all of the walls—even on the second floor, a rarity in those days. The furniture was mostly, appropriately, American-made, but porcelains, silver, and glassware were imported from Europe.

President Washington was criticized for his lifestyle, which was, indeed, a cut above the average American's, and he responded by refusing to accept a salary. In lieu of a paycheck, he was awarded $25,000 a year for expenses. He and his wife, Martha, spent most of it on their house, and a precedent was

established allowing former presidents to take some of the furnishings with them when they moved out of the official residence.

The Washingtons moved from their first New York house a little more than a year after moving into it. The second official presidential home was on Broadway right around the corner from the building on Wall Street where the government was headquartered. The new house had been the residence of the French minister, and Washington saved him the bother of shipping his furnishings home by buying it all. The style of the presidency changed overnight.

In another year, the government moved from New York, and the Washingtons moved along with it.

A decision had been made to establish the national capital to a ten-mile-square (640,000m²) site on the Potomac River, but in the meantime, the government relocated to Philadelphia while it was being built. During their time as Philadelphians, the Washington

family lived at 190 High Street, the former home of Robert Morris. The house was altered to reflect its new use, but the president preferred to furnish it with the things he had brought from New York. He said he was pleased with how well the new house accommodated his furniture. He was so pleased, in fact, that he refused an offer by the State of Pennsylvania to build him a new one. He and his family lived there for seven years until his second term ended in 1797.

His successor, John Adams, and his wife Abigail, moved in after his inauguration, but before his term of office ended, they shipped their worldly goods to the new capital city and established residence in a still-unfinished building there called the President's Mansion.

THE FEDERAL CITY

Even before the federal government established itself in New York City, lawmakers were looking at alternate sites. They liked New York well enough, but even in 1789 the pace was

Both George Washington and John Adams lived in a house on Ninth Street in Philadelphia during most of their presidential years. In spite of an offer by the State of Pennsylvania to give them this roomier mansion, they were content to stay there.

During his years in New York and Philadelphia, Washington acquired this Federal Period chair, which eventually found its way into the White House, even if he himself didn't.

a bit fast for them. And the southerners among them, especially, wanted the center of government a little closer to home.

There were several eager contenders, but once the decision to move was made, it was generally conceded that they'd go to Philadelphia. It was where it all began, after all, and former members of the Continental Congress gravitated there like cows to the barn at the end of the day. In fact, after the Revolutionary War ended, the new Constitution was drafted and debated in Philadelphia, then sent to the states for ratification in 1787, and before the government moved to New York with the inauguration of its first president two years later, Congress convened in Philadelphia, without giving a second thought to any other possible location.

They hadn't thought about the fact that their constituents also considered it a logical place to take their grievances, though. Not long after Congress established itself there, a gaggle of Revolutionary War veterans set up camp outside the State House demanding back pay. The lawmakers called out the militia, but nobody responded, so they solved the problem by leaving town.

They went all the way up to Princeton, New Jersey, but when the snows began to fly, they moved to the more hospitable climate of Annapolis, Maryland, and then went back north to Trenton, New Jersey. They eventually wound up in New York, and when it was proposed, they eagerly bought into the president's plan to build a whole new capital near his Mount Vernon plantation.

Apparently forgetting all about those veterans, they also agreed to relocate to Philadelphia for the ten years it would take this new Federal City to rise from the wilderness.

GETTING IT TOGETHER

It takes money to build a city from scratch, and the young government was woefully short of it. Because of that, the original plan called for nothing more than a Capitol Building, a Navy

Yard, and a President's Palace. But the budgeteers had overlooked the fact that the local planters expected to be paid for their fields and farms and for their houses. The President himself had to wade personally into that problem.

He invited his former neighbors for an evening of drinking and good cheer at a Georgetown tavern, and the next morning, most of them had only fuzzy memories of the arm-twisting that took place. They were stunned to realize that they had agreed to accept $66 an acre for land earmarked for public buildings, but nothing at all for land that would be used for streets and boulevards.

Taken as a patriotic gesture, though, it didn't seem like a bad deal. They had been entertained by the President himself, the wine was good, and none of them was in danger of losing all of his land, which would leave them at the center of the action in years to come.

A few of them began to get a little squeamish a few days later when an odd-looking little man with surveyor's equipment began traipsing across their land. He was deciding where the streets would go, and that made them nervous. The man was Major Pierre Charles L'Enfant, a hero of the late war, who had designed New York's Federal Hall, and now had been hired by the President to lay out the new city. "But he's from Paris," they whispered, "and the Champs Elysée is the widest boulevard in the whole world. Suppose he likes that sort of thing." Others pointed out that his father had been a gardener at Versailles. "Do big fancy parks and gardens qualify as thoroughfares?" If so, they knew it was going to cost them a lot of donated land.

They grumbled among themselves for months as the engineer got in the way of their fox hunts. Finally, they invited President Washington back to Georgetown for some more wine and some more information. They didn't like what they heard. The plan Washington showed them covered 6,611 acres (2,677ha), of which 541 (219ha) were to be the sites of public buildings. The rest, 3,600 acres (1,458ha), was earmarked for streets and avenues.

Then the President smiled and took a sip from his wine glass. Add 3,600 and 541, and you account for 4,141 acres (1,677ha), he told them. The balance of the land covered by the plan came to 2,470 acres (1,000ha), which, he told these landowners, they would

L ENFANT

Although he wasn't very popular among the local gentry, Pierre Charles L'Enfant deserves all the credit for the plan of the city that became Washington, D.C.

L'Enfant was also the designer of New York's City Hall, where President Washington took his first oath of office. A few years later, it was torn down and sold for scrap. Its replacement, now called Federal Hall, has become a Wall Street landmark.

be free to sell off as commercial property. Well, almost free. Washington noted that since the federal government would hold title to the whole tract, it would keep half the proceeds of any sales, with the original owner pocketing the other half.

Disappointed as they may have been, they all realized that their half would be worth hundreds more than the $66 an acre they had agreed to for public buildings. They accepted the offer and signed a contract. With that, the concept of a Federal City became official on the last day of June in 1791.

THE PLAN

L'Enfant had been turning over a plan for the city in his mind for more than three years by then. Although he had been hired by Washington, a former surveyor, and was, in theory, working with Thomas Jefferson, an amateur architect, neither of them gave him any idea of what they might have had in mind.

That was just fine with L'Enfant, who wasn't too keen on supervision, anyway, and considered himself one of the great artists of his day. His weakest point, though, was that he didn't know a thing about politics, and didn't care. That would come back to haunt him.

When he showed the first draft of his plan to Washington and Jefferson, the President, probably with his former neighbors in mind, suggested that maybe so many wide avenues might be gilding the lily a bit. Jefferson suggested that a mall might be nice. He also added the idea that streets ought to be numbered alphabetically east and west from the Capitol, and numerically north and south of it.

L'Enfant followed their suggestions, but in the end the plan was almost completely his own. He included the traditional grid pattern of streets meeting at right angles to one another, and he broke their monotony with radial roads that created a series of plazas that opened up sweeping vistas. He also used many of the

L'Enfant's original plan for the Federal City, which kept mysteriously disappearing just before land auctions were held, has badly faded over the years, but any map of present-day Washington will fill in the gaps. It wasn't changed much from drawing to execution.

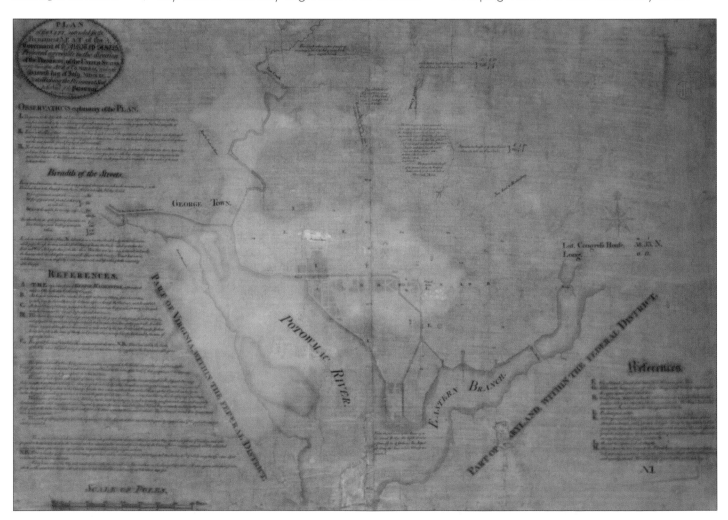

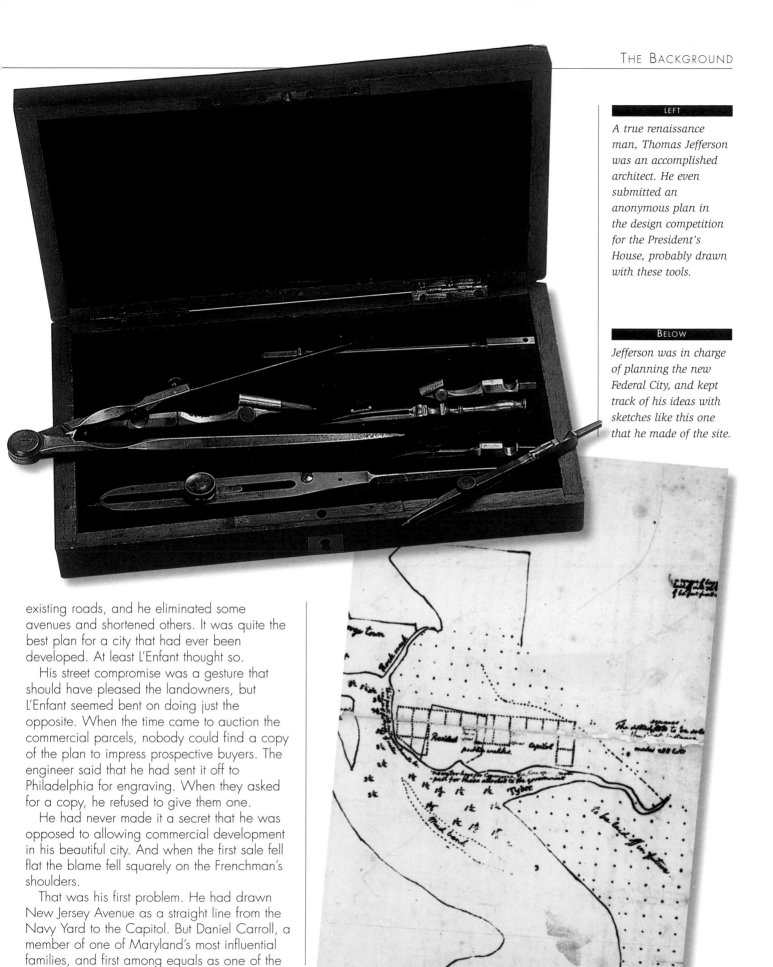

A true renaissance man, Thomas Jefferson was an accomplished architect. He even submitted an anonymous plan in the design competition for the President's House, probably drawn with these tools.

Jefferson was in charge of planning the new Federal City, and kept track of his ideas with sketches like this one that he made of the site.

existing roads, and he eliminated some avenues and shortened others. It was quite the best plan for a city that had ever been developed. At least L'Enfant thought so.

His street compromise was a gesture that should have pleased the landowners, but L'Enfant seemed bent on doing just the opposite. When the time came to auction the commercial parcels, nobody could find a copy of the plan to impress prospective buyers. The engineer said that he had sent it off to Philadelphia for engraving. When they asked for a copy, he refused to give them one.

He had never made it a secret that he was opposed to allowing commercial development in his beautiful city. And when the first sale fell flat the blame fell squarely on the Frenchman's shoulders.

That was his first problem. He had drawn New Jersey Avenue as a straight line from the Navy Yard to the Capitol. But Daniel Carroll, a member of one of Maryland's most influential families, and first among equals as one of the

CAPITOL SITE SELECTION · 1791

Although he had no patience with politics, L'Enfant made it a point to keep President Washington informed of his plans every step of the way.

Daniel Carroll, the son of a signer of the Declaration of Independence, was one of the original landowners in the tract that became the Federal City. He was influential in having L'Enfant fired.

The original plan included streets meeting at right angles, but softened the grid with plazas and avenues radiating from them that provided vistas in nearly every part of the city.

local landowners, was building a manor house right in the middle of that line. He had begun construction long before the plan was made, and said that he had talked L'Enfant into making the avenue a little narrower at that point. L'Enfant said he had never promised any such thing and sent a crew out to tear down the Carroll Manor.

President Washington agreed to pay for the physical damage, but there wasn't any way to compensate Daniel Carroll for the injury to his pride. L'Enfant didn't help a bit when he refused to apologize. "It would set a dangerous precedent," he huffed.

Then, as if to prove just how dangerous this precedent could be, when another land auction was scheduled, L'Enfant sent his plan back to the Philadelphia engraver. Without it, buyers had no clue what they were bidding on and opted not to bid on anything.

That was the last straw. One month short of a year since he began the job, Major Pierre Charles L'Enfant was fired. But his plan was in place and it wasn't changed much as construction went slowly forward. Of all the men who have made their mark on Washington, D.C., where politics and compromise are usually all that matters, the most lasting impression was made by this man who would rather have died than compromise, and considered politics a dirty word.

Who knows? If he hadn't been so stubborn, L'Enfant might have been the architect of the White House and not just its glorious surroundings.

THE PRESIDENTIAL PALACE

L'Enfant had, indeed, sketched out a proposal for the president's house. He called it the Presidential Palace, and his plan called for a building that was as palatial as any in the world. Washington, although he knew that he would never live there himself, was ecstatic about it. Who wouldn't be? L'Enfant's scheme called for a massive stone building that would measure 700 by 200 feet (213 by 61m)—not as big as Versailles, but right up there among the great palaces of Europe. Without consulting with anyone, he even ordered work to begin on the building's foundations.

Meanwhile, the American government, new as it was, had divided itself into two warring camps. The Federalists, who were represented by Washington himself, were foursquare on the side of a strong central government run by a rich ruling class. On the other side were the Antifederalists, who believed in giving a voice to farmers and others; they would be called commoners back in the Old Country. Their leader was Thomas Jefferson, who was actually in charge of developing the new Federal City.

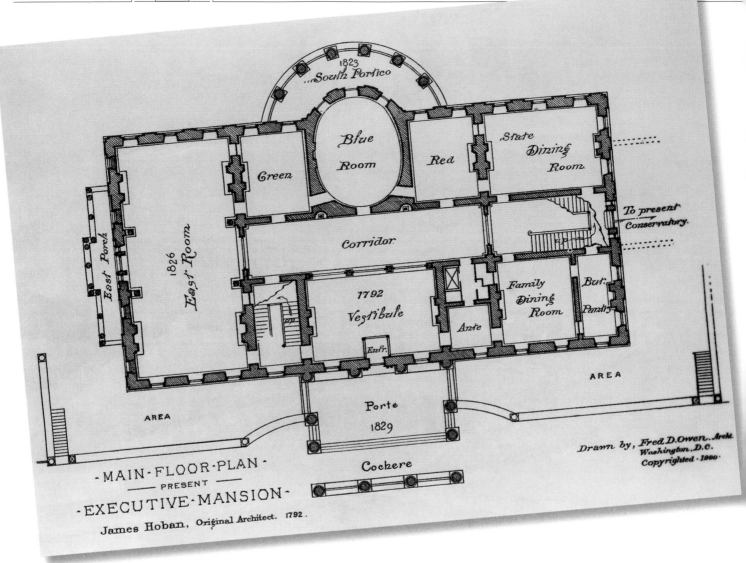

1823
...South Portico...

Blue
Room

Red

State
Dining
Room

Green

East Porch

1826
East Room

Corridor

To present
Conservatory.

1792
Vestibule

Family
Dining
Room

But.
Pantry

Ante

AREA

Ent.r.

AREA

Porte
1829

Drawn by, Fred. D. Owen, Archt.
Washington, D.C.
Copyrighted · 1900

·MAIN·FLOOR·PLAN·
—— PRESENT ——
·EXECUTIVE·MANSION·

Cochere

James Hoban, Original Architect. 1792.

ABOVE

James Hoban's original ground floor plan for the Executive Mansion has been changed quite a bit over the years. This version of it reflects the changes that were made during Theodore Roosevelt's administration.

Jefferson was willing to look the other way when L'Enfant proposed wide boulevards and fountain-filled plazas. He thought it was a bit grand for a country of yeoman farmers, but he loved Paris, possibly more than any other American-born citizen, and agreed with the Parisian-inspired ideas he saw on paper.

But that Presidential Palace, in his view, went too far. It smacked of royalty, and that, after all, was what the Revolutionary War had been fought to drive out of America. Although Jefferson was in charge, L'Enfant had the President's ear, and he knew he would be overruled. Thomas Jefferson was a very happy man the day L'Enfant was fired.

With the original architect out of the picture, Jefferson suggested a design competition for the Capitol Building and for the President's House. The prize for the best executive mansion design would be either a gold medal or $500 and, of

course, the honor of the architectural commission. There were nine entries, including an anonymous one that seems to have been the work of Thomas Jefferson himself.

Washington personally chose the winner, an Irish architect named James Hoban. His scheme for a three-story stone building was officially approved by the Board of Commissioners in the summer of 1792 with the comment that the plan was, "convenient, elegant and within a moderate expence [sic]."

Then the President began having second thoughts. He didn't think the mansion would be big enough to meet the needs of future presidents, and he ordered an expansion, along with a more elaborate facade that would be embellished with stone carvings. Even a president can be overruled, though, and the commissioners balked at what all this was going to cost. Washington compromised by

agreeing to eliminate the third floor. Still not completely satisfied, the commissioners decided to build the house of brick covered with stone, rather than the original all-stone construction Hoban had proposed. It all helped to bring the budget in line, but the President's House still wound up costing in the neighborhood of $300,000.

THE WORK BEGUN

Later that summer, the President and the architect met on the site itself. As a former surveyor, Washington had no problem visualizing what was to come. But there was a problem. L'Enfant's palace had been sited on a direct line with the Capitol Building up Pennsylvania Avenue, but this new plan called for a considerably smaller building—even though it was still the biggest residence anywhere in America—that would be set back from the axis. Washington had to decide exactly *where* it would sit, and where it would face.

The spot he chose was on a steep hillside sloping down to the Potomac River. It wasn't exactly on the Classical axis called for in the original plan, but in the end, it was much better.

Work actually began in the early fall of 1792, with James Hoban, the architect,

White House architect James Hoban was honored with his likeness on a postage stamp, but at eighteen cents, it isn't likely it achieved a wide circulation.

Of all the parts of the White House that have been altered over the years, none has been changed as much as the second floor where the First Family actually lives. This version was for Roosevelt's big family.

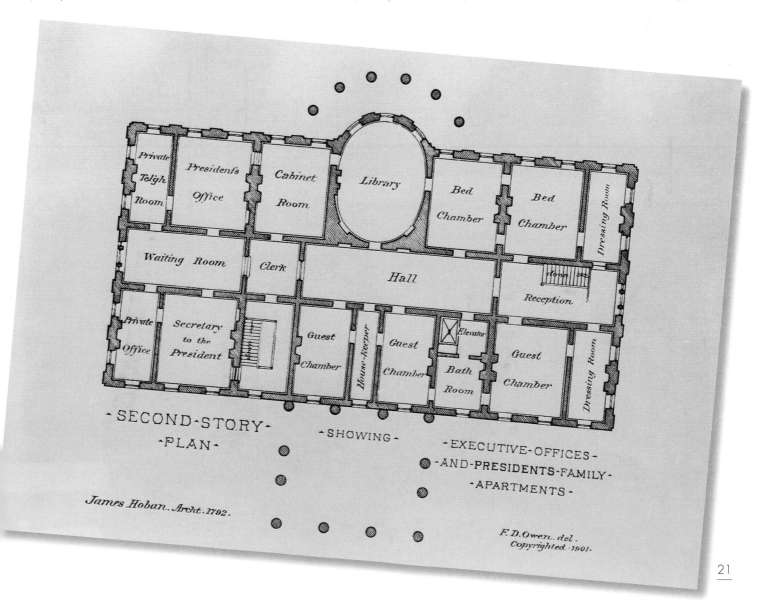

stonecutters were especially in short supply. Frustrated, the commissioners opened their purse strings a little, and approved importing a few master stonecutters from Scotland. The first of them didn't show up on the job until 1794. Two of the eight years they thought they had to meet their deadline were lost. The sandstone they worked with was quarried in Virginia, about forty miles (64km) away, but the bricks that were used were made from the soil on the site, which was a mix of sand and clay—perfect for brickmaking.

The problem was that the commissioners had specified brick for the inner walls of all of the other buildings that were being built in the city at the time, and that added up to hundreds of tons of bricks. The brickmakers worked as fast as they could, but it never seemed to be fast enough. The process was time-consuming. They dug the raw materials from pits on the property, then they combined the clay and sand with water and packed the mix into wooden molds. After that, the raw bricks needed to be thoroughly dried and then fired in kilns. Fortunately, the bricks they made were for interior walls and didn't need to be fired to maximum hardness. But it all took time, and time was in short supply.

ABOVE

Modern presidents are photographed every couple of minutes, but earlier ones, like George Washington, had to sit for hours to have their portraits painted.

RIGHT

Each of the bricks used in the building of the President's House had to be made by hand from materials found on the site itself.

serving as supervisor of construction. Thanks to L'Enfant's earlier foundation work, which because of its size spilled over to the new site, excavation was relatively easy, and in less than a month it was time to lay the cornerstone. After a great deal of ceremony and quite a bit of speechmaking, master mason Collen Williamson fastened a brass plate to the top of a foundation stone at the southwest corner at the rear of the house.

The plate was engraved with the words, "This first stone of the President's House was laid on the 13th day of October, 1792, and in the seventeenth year of the independence of the United States of America." The inscription was followed by the names of the architect, the commissioners, the stonemason, and, of course, the President who would never get to live there.

In the meantime, the legislation that had created this Federal City had set a deadline of December 1800, for the establishment of the government there. Although the deadline was slightly more than eight years away, it was a busy time for all the construction trades. But

Among the personal effects George Washington left behind are (clockwise from top left): a fingerbowl made in Bristol, England, of blown glass; a French-made porcelain saucer, polychrome enameled and gilded; a tea bowl matching the saucer; a pewter and steel shoe buckle; a comb with matching case made of horn; a jewel used in Freemasonry ritual (thought to have been worn by George Washington at the Fredericksburg Masonic Lodge No. 4); a snuff box made of paper maché, tortoiseshell, and printed paper, made in either England or France; and an elegantly engraved, hand-blown wineglass, probably made in England. As a wealthy Virginia planter, Washington had a lifestyle that was a cut above most Americans of his day. Many of these items were gifts from admirers, some of whom lived in other countries.

ABOVE

A modified plan of the Federal City, made three years after the L'Enfant original, shows the locations of the Capitol and the President's House. The mansion was moved slightly from its original position.

Still, in those days, construction was a seasonal affair, and the job was shut down during the winter months. But by then, the basement, which is above ground level, was already finished, and three-foot-thick (91-cm) walls rose up to a height of thirteen feet (4m). The building's outer dimensions, well defined by then, measured 168 by 85 feet (51 by 26m). It was a far cry from L'Enfant's dream of a palace, but sidewalk superintendents who lived nearby were very much impressed.

Quite a bit was finished behind those walls, too. In those short fall months, all of the supports for the basement's ceiling had been put in place, as well as most of the stone arches that would eventually support the finished building. But there was still a lot that needed to be done, and the President was putting the pressure on. As the final year of his presidency approached, his political enemies stepped up their criticism of what they perceived to be his elitist attitude and the

President's House became the focal point of their carping. To make their point, they began sarcastically calling it a "palace" again.

Washington knew that his successor might possibly be from that other faction, and he was determined to make certain that both the Capitol Building and the President's House were too far along to be changed after he stepped down. He didn't expect that either building could be finished by the time he went back to Mount Vernon, but he made it clear

that he wanted everybody to start working a little harder.

The commissioners offered a compromise. In order to speed up the construction of the Capitol Building, they said, they would put a temporary roof on the President's House and send every available worker up to the Capitol.

In the mystique that has grown up around the memory of George Washington, it is easy to assume that he was a mild-mannered man who rarely, if ever, lost his temper. But this is one recorded instance of a time when he did. The President literally hit the ceiling when he was told of the commissioners' idea. "It was not, and is not, my intention that the work on that house should cease," he thundered. It didn't.

By the time Washington's presidency ended in 1797, the house still wasn't finished, but construction had passed the point of no return. The walls were in place, although the windows were not, and the roof was framed but uncovered. It seemed highly likely that it might be finished by the December 1800, deadline.

It was, in fact, declared habitable in time for President John Adams to take possession of it two months early. By that time, nobody thought of calling this place the Federal City anymore. It had been known as Washington almost from the start, and only the President himself shied away from calling it that. When he retired from the presidency, though, even he called it Washington.

The Capitol Building was originally designed by Dr. William Thornton, an amateur architect, who won a design competition with this design and was given $500 as well as a city lot.

Even as it was being built, the President's House was a major tourist attraction in the new city. Sidewalk superintendants watched carefully as each stone was set in place.

2 The House as a Home

John Adams had been President for three years before he and his wife, Abigail, moved down to Washington. During all that time, he had shown almost no interest in the new city, nor in the house that was being built for him and his successors. He had only seen it once before actually moving into it.

John Adam's prayer for the house is engraved on a mantel in the State Dining Room.

After it was torched in 1814, nothing but a charred shell remained of the President's House, much of which needed to be torn down.

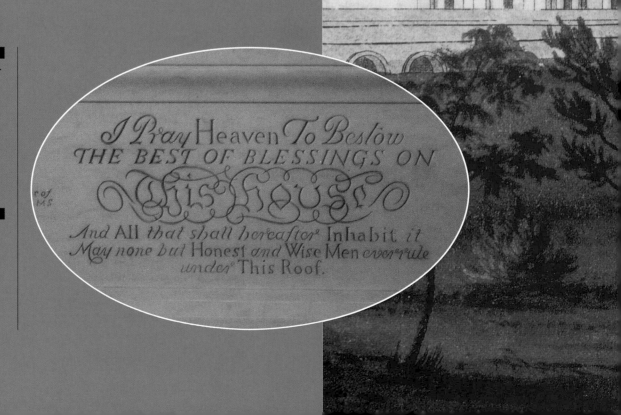

I Pray Heaven To Bestow THE BEST OF BLESSINGS ON This House And All that shall hereafter Inhabit it May none but Honest and Wise Men ever rule under This Roof.

26

A letter from President Adams gave government officials just thirty days to move from Philadelphia and get their departments up and running in the new Federal City.

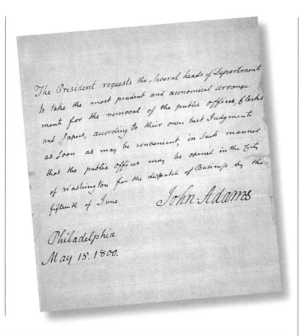

The President requests the several heads of Departments to take the most prudent and œconomical arrangement for the removal of the public offices, Clerks and Papers, according to their own best Judgment as soon as may be convenient, in such manner that the public offices may be opened in the City of Washington for the despatch of Business by the fifteenth of June

John Adams

*Philadelphia
May 15ᵗʰ. 1800.*

John Singleton Copley's portrait of John Adams captures the note of formality the President preferred.

When he finally arrived there, nobody was expecting him and he wandered through the still-unfinished rooms alone, except for the servants who were unpacking his furniture. The place left a lot to be desired, but when he wrote a letter to his wife about his first day in the President's House, he didn't say much about what he thought of it, except that she would soon be able to "form the best idea of it" on her own.

He closed the letter with a thought that a later President, Franklin D. Roosevelt, would have engraved on a plaque that is mounted on a fireplace mantle in the State Dining Room: "I pray heaven to bestow the best of blessings on this house and all that shall hereafter inhabit it. May none but honest and wise men ever rule under this roof."

When Abigail finally did arrive, her "best idea" of the place was none too good. "We have indeed come into a new country," she wrote. The grounds were a mess, littered with debris, tools, ditches, and workmen's sheds. The only way to get into the house was up a rickety wooden staircase, and inside the only way to get upstairs was a narrow stairway that was intended for servants. The Adams family had had thirty servants in Philadelphia, but Abigail was informed that there was no budget for anything like that in Washington, and she was forced to make do with the four she had brought with her.

But Abigail Adams didn't lack for company. Construction was still going on, and although she was appalled at the slowness of these southerners compared to workmen back home in Massachusetts, she was happy that anything at all was being accomplished. Lacking any better space, she used the Audience Room, later to be called the East Room, as a place to hang out clothes to dry. The water to wash the clothes had to be carried in buckets from the nearest well half a mile away.

The Adamses were not rich, but they managed to scrape the money together for the entertaining that was required of them, and to buy furniture for this huge mansion that was a far cry from the little saltbox house they called home back in Massachusetts. "I expect to be obliged to resign in six months," the President wrote of his financial distress. But he would only have to put up with it for three months. Thomas Jefferson would defeat him in the election of 1800, and he was evicted from the

White House the following March. Not too fond of his successor at the time, Adams avoided Jefferson's inauguration by slipping away at four in the morning. Abigail had already left weeks earlier to avoid the inconveniences of traveling during the spring thaw.

THE JEFFERSON YEARS

Thomas Jefferson took his time moving into the White House. More than two weeks passed between the time he took the oath of office, and darkened the doors of his new home. He was apparently happy at the boarding house where he had been living. At least it was finished.

Actually, he used the time to have some changes made in the President's House. He ordered a well dug, for instance, and he asked

to have the outhouse torn down. He also installed an underground wine cellar. Then he turned his attention to the interior. He reconfigured the way guests would be received by having the recently finished stairways removed from what is now the Blue Room, and building new ones on the north side of the house where guests could assemble in a large hall.

He turned the levee room into his library and abolished the custom of levees, an early day version of the cocktail party, much to the consternation of local Society. In fact, he banished the custom of party-giving almost completely, reducing the list of functions and balls to New Year's Day and the Fourth of July. There were no invitations to either of them, and anybody willing to slosh through muddy, unfinished roads was welcome to come. Jefferson also abolished the custom of bowing to his guests, as both Washington and Adams had done, in favor of shaking their hands. He

insisted on being called Mr. Jefferson, and not "Mr. President."

The Fourth of July celebrations had all the earmarks of a country fair. There were cockfights and dog fights staged on the lawn, and vendors sold food to people who had traveled from every part of the country to take part in the festivities. A highlight was the appearance of the President at the front door, followed by an invitation to go inside for a glass of wine, or punch, and other light refreshments.

The President's House had been transformed into the "People's House."

When the British minister presented himself there, the President greeted him in a dressing gown and slippers. It shocked the man, who reported, "I found myself... introduced to a man as President of the United States, not merely in undress, but *actually standing in slippers down at the heels*, and both pantaloons, coat, and under-clothes indicative

The mural, "Three Great Men," by Constantino Brumaldi, represents President George Washington consulting with his Seretary of State, Thomas Jefferson, and Secretary of the Treasury, Alexander Hamilton.

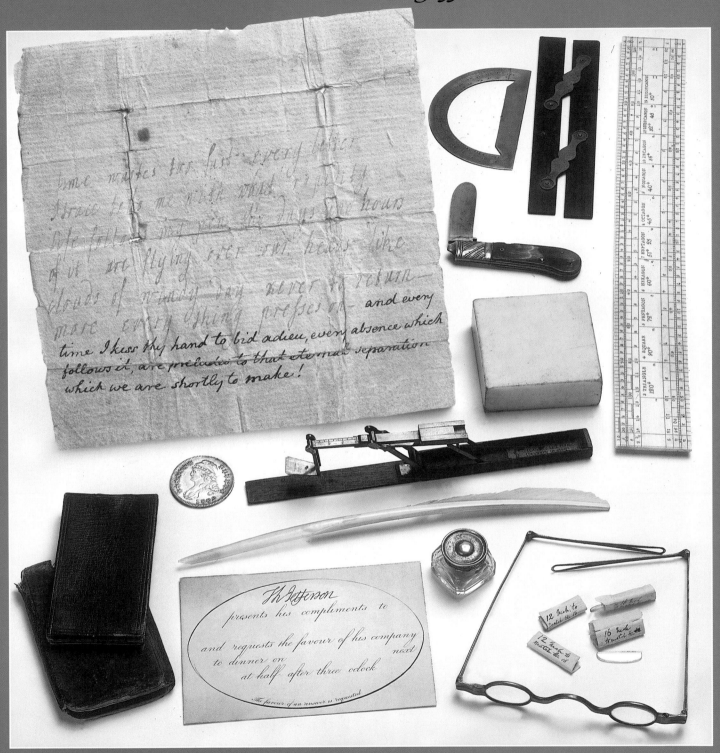

Thomas Jefferson's personal effects include (clockwise from top left): A handwritten copy of an excerpt from Laurence Sterne's poem, "Tristram Shandy," intended as a tribute to his late wife, Martha, who died after giving birth to their sixth child; drafting tools, including a protractor, paralellogram and sliderule—Jefferson's collection of mathematical apparatus, acquired from the best London manufacturers, was one of the finest in the country; a folding pocketknife; pocket scales, made in Kirkby, near Liverpool, England; a quill pen; folding spectacles; a set of bifocal lenses wrapped in papers; an inkwell; a blank dinner invitation; and a leather-bound pocket diary and its slipcase. Among Jefferson's most-prized possessions was a fiddle, which he played to relax from the activity of his other endless interests.

One of Thomas Jefferson's early drawings for Monticello, the Virginia home he designed for himself, shows that the plan didn't just leap from his mind. The upper row of colonnades and the triangular pediment were replaced by a Classical dome.

of utter slovenliness and indifference to appearances."

Although formality was never far from the surface, for the next hundred years it was possible for anyone at all to walk up to the White House door unannounced and uninvited and have a fairly good chance of having a chat with the president, whether he was dressed for the occasion or not. As late as the 1920s, President Harding often answered the door himself.

When Jefferson moved in, there were no ancillary buildings on the site—except for the outhouse. He changed that in 1808 by designing a pair of wings, similar to those at his home, Monticello, in Virginia. The predecessors of today's East and West Wings, they were flat-roofed colonnaded spaces that were filled with such things as stables and henhouses, servant's quarters, and the icehouse.

The President's House had been transformed into a decent place to live.

THE FIRE

Jefferson's wife had died before he became president, and when he needed an official

hostess, he often called on Dolley Madison, the wife of his friend James Madison. When she became First Lady in her own right, she was already quite familiar with the drill. Her husband, the fourth president, also knew his way around the mansion where he had worked as Jefferson's secretary of state.

When they moved in, though, the house wasn't quite the same as they remembered it. Most of the furniture had been carted back to Monticello, and most of what was left behind was in a sorry state. Dolley already knew what she was going to find in the china closets and silver drawers. Just about everything there had been showing signs of wear for years, and she wasn't too surprised by the condition of the other things Jefferson had left behind. But she wasn't at all shy about asking for help. She invited a congressional delegation to tour the house with her and within weeks they appropriated $12,000 for general repairs and another $14,000 for new furnishings.

The Madisons also did a little fixing up on their own. Jefferson's library was converted back to the State Dining Room, and Dolley spruced up the parlor, now called the Red

Room, and the oval drawing room, which became known as the Blue Room. She introduced a Classical Greek style, over the ever-popular French, in the furnishings. Nearly everything that she bought came from American merchants, but patriotism had nothing to do with it. British warships had bottled up American ports and anything imported was out of the question.

British actions in the west led to a declaration of war, but the English were also at war with France at the time, and it wasn't until 1814, when that phase ended, that the so-called War of 1812 hit America hardest. In the summer of 1814, British troops came ashore north of Washington and began marching on the city. Madison surrounded the President's House with militia and urged Dolley to leave town. But in spite of British boasts that they intended to take her prisoner, she refused to go. "I am determined to stay with my husband," she announced.

Her husband didn't stay with her, as it turned out, and he was off at the front lines when the enemy came in sight. Dolley had already packed two small trunks with papers and a change of clothes, and when the militia finally

James Madison never wore anything but black clothes, prompting a friend to describe him as looking like "a schoolmaster dressed for a funeral."

On August 24, 1814, British troops marched on Washington bent on burning down the whole city. They might have succeeded, but a hurricane blew in before they could finish.

ABOVE

As she was leaving the
mansion under attack,
Dolley Madison had a
servant break the frame
and remove Gilbert
Stuart's portrait of
George Washington,
which she entrusted
to two vistors for
safekeeping.

RIGHT

The full-length
Washington portrait
was the first work of art
purchased for the
President's House in
1800, and originally
hung in the Blue Room,
then the President's
Drawing Room. Today
it is in the East Room.

34

ordered her to leave, she rushed through the house gathering up other things that she thought ought to be saved. Among them were silver, some books, some curtains and the already priceless Gilbert Stuart portrait of Washington that was hanging in the State Dining Room.

Her husband, the President, arrived back a half-hour after she left at three in the morning, but it wasn't until evening that the British themselves arrived. By then the house was empty and Madison had fled to the safety of the French minister's residence, Dolley's caged pet macaw in hand.

The British Admiral, George Cockburn, and his men sat down to a leisurely dinner, which seemed to have been spread out for them. After cautioning his men against looting (which they did anyway), he ordered them to push all the furniture into the center of the rooms and then smash all the windows. About fifty more troops outside were armed with long poles with oil-soaked cotton batting on the end, and on a signal, they set fire to the cotton and pushed it through the broken windows. The whole building was enveloped in flames almost instantaneously.

As if as a sign from God, a hurricane struck Washington the next morning. The downpour put out the fire, and the high winds sent the invaders back to secure their ships. They sailed off soon afterward without the First Lady as their prisoner. When she and her husband arrived back at their home, they found nothing but a charred shell. The roof had been completely burned away, and the interior reduced to ashes. The Capitol Building had also been struck during the attack. Its pillars were cracked and broken, and its dome had crashed down into the cellar. Rebuilding it was delayed while Congress debated the wisdom of moving its base of operations to an entirely different city.

The President, meanwhile, didn't wait for the debating to end. He ordered an immediate rebuilding of the destroyed mansion, and insisted that it should be restored exactly as it had been. To help ensure that, James Hoban, the original architect, was called back to supervise the reconstruction.

The stone of the walls had cracked in the heat and the sudden cooling by the rain. The interior brick walls were crumbling, too, and Hoban reached the conclusion that most of the

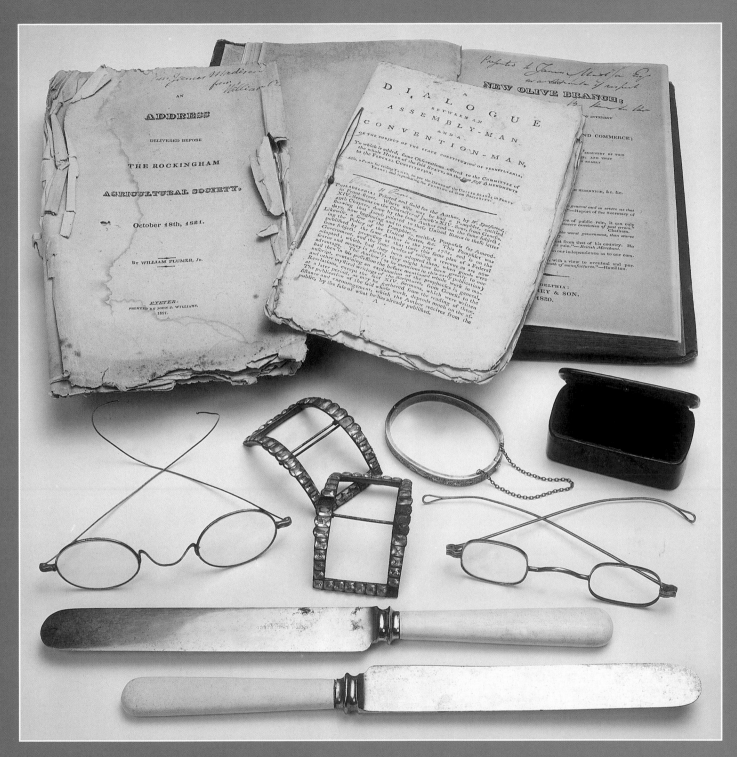

The personal effects of James and Dolley Madison include (clockwise from top left): A copy of an address by William Plummer, Jr. on October 18, 1821, to the Rockingham Agricultural Society, inscribed to Madison, who himself was president of the Albemarle Agricultural Society; a copy of "A Dialogue Between an Assembly-Man and a Convention-man on the Subject of the State Constitution of Pennsylvania;" a printed copy of The New Olive Branch, signed for James Madison by its author, William Plumer, Jr.; an imitation tortoiseshell snuff box owned by Dolley Madison; knives from the family's silver service; James Madison's spectacles; shoe buckles with imitation jewels; and Dolley Madison's gold bracelet. After leaving the White House, the Madisons retired to their Virginia home, Montpelier.

James Monroe, who had fought in the Revolution, always dressed in the spirit of '76, even though styles had changed by the time he became president in 1817.

Reconstruction of the Executive Mansion was still underway when Monroe took office. He gave the builders an eight-month deadline, and demanded weekly progress reports.

walls would have to be torn down and completely replaced.

By 1817, when James Monroe became the next president, the walls had been restored, the roof replaced, and work was going forward on the interior. The new stone was sealed with white lead paint and what black scars were left disappeared. The building that had taken close to ten years to build was rebuilt in less than three. It was reopened by President Monroe for a New Year's party in 1818, even though the paint hadn't dried yet.

He christened it the "Executive Mansion" that day. It had a better ring to it than "President's House," and no one would think of calling it the "White House" for another hundred years. That was the brainchild of Theodore Roosevelt, who pointed out that every state in the Union had an Executive Mansion.

FURNISHING THE SHELL

When the Monroes moved in, the only furnishing in the mansion was the Gilbert Stuart portrait that Dolley Madison had saved. Congress agreed to buy the family's personal furniture for a little more than $9,000, although it took them five years to come across with the money.

The government also appropriated $20,000 to buy new furniture. Monroe's taste was for French styles, and when he had furniture

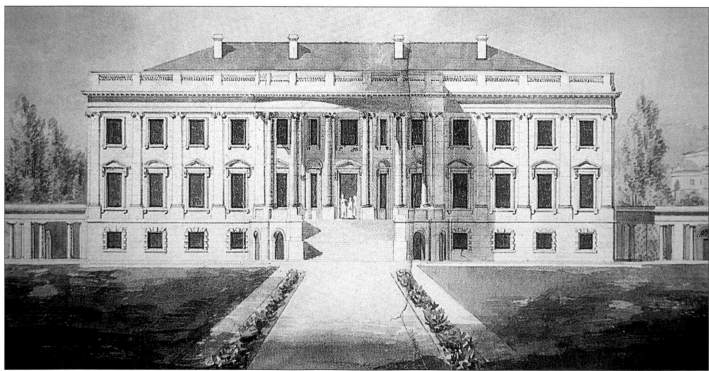

The personal effects of President James Monroe include (clockwise from top left):

A porcelain saucer used in the Monroe White House; a key to the mansion's front door; a steel-framed folding magnifying glass; a red leather-bound razor strop, presented to President Monroe on July 4, 1823; a brass pocket compass; a pair of English flintlock pocket pistols made by Hewson in Exeter, England; a pair of doeskin gloves; silver riding spurs; a pair of silver-framed spectacles, with adjustable stems, and their case; a gold-cased pocket watch with its key, marked "Gabriel, London"; a brass pocket telescope; and a silver-mounted folding straight razor with tortoiseshell handle, probably made in England. Although he came from humble beginnings as the son of a carpenter, Monroe made it a point to live like a gentleman, even when he couldn't afford to.

shipped from France, American manufacturers raised a protest. Monroe shrugged it off by pointing out the house was intended to impress foreign ministers. These purchases will make them feel right at home, he said.

Foreign relations had only recently become an American concern. The end of the war with England had made America an equal partner with Britain in world trade, and the world was beginning to look at this upstart country with a little more respect. The war's end also brought unprecedented prosperity to the country, and Congress generously came up with another grant—$30,000—to buy more furniture for the Executive Mansion. This time, Madison spent the money on American-made furnishings, telling his benefactors that he was buying with an eye to the future. They will last, he wrote to Congress, "...with care, more than twenty, and some of them, perhaps fifty years." His prediction proved to be way off the mark. Some of the things he bought have lasted 185 years, and are still among the house's greatest treasures.

THE PEOPLE'S HOUSE

After Andrew Jackson took the oath of office as President, it took him more than an hour to make his way down Pennsylvania Avenue from the Capitol to the Executive Mansion. The biggest crowds Washington had ever seen

converged on the city to celebrate the fact that one of their own had finally been elected. And even when he finally made it to the front gate of his new home, he had to wade through a sea of enthusiastic humanity that had assembled on the lawn.

When Jackson finally made it to the Oval Room to receive his guests, he was pushed up against a wall, gasping for air. Aides set up a phalanx around him, and he was carried out through a window and into a waiting carriage that sped him away from the crowd. It was said that nobody noticed that the President wasn't there for his party.

In an attempt to get the well-wishers out of the house, refreshments were set up out on the lawn. But it was too little, too late. In the crush, the mob had broken thousands of dollars-worth of china and glassware, tracked mud onto the carpets, and broke a great deal of the fragile furniture. One eyewitness to the spectacle reported that the crowd included "all sorts of people, from the highest and

most polished, down to the most vulgar and gross." But together they represented the People, and this was their house, too. It was the first time most Americans looked at it that way.

Andrew Jackson, with the possible exception of George Washington, may have been the most popular of any of America's presidents. Although, like Washington, he was a wealthy southern planter, he was regarded by nearly everybody except the Northeastern Establishment as a true "Man of the People." He earned the nickname "Old Hickory" as the commander who beat the British in the Battle of New Orleans, the last battle of the War of 1812, and he attracted some attention as a rough and ready frontiersman, Indian fighter, brawler, and for his frequent defense of his family's honor on the dueling field.

Little had been done in the way of expansion or refurnishing during the time John Quincy Adams, Jackson's predecessor, lived in the house. But Jackson didn't waste any time in making up for lost time. Part of the original

ABOVE

Although well known and well respected in the South, Jackson became a national hero by winning the Battle of New Orleans, the last of the War of 1812. Just before the battle, the British Admiral boasted that, "I shall eat my Christmas dinner in New Orleans." Jackson shot back, "But I shall have the honor of presiding at that dinner."

As soon as Jackson arrived, work began on building the North Portico, which had been part of the original plan, but had been delayed time and again for lack of funds. Although a would-be-assassin had attacked Jackson, there was no security in place at the Mansion. The doors were left unlocked and the streets around it left unpatroled.

Peggy O'Neale Eaton, wife of Jackson's war secretary, scandalized Washington society because of her "common" background. But Jackson called her accusers to a Cabinet meeting to argue their case. When they had finished, he pronounced her "chaste as a virgin," and the case was closed.

plan, but still unbuilt, was the north portico, and he started there. The result was a rectangular porch over the main entrance supported by fifty-foot (127-m) columns. In addition to the columned portico that extended out over the driveway, he also ordered the stone gates on Pennsylvania Avenue set further apart to make it easier for carriages to negotiate the turn onto the grounds.

Jackson also expanded the mansion's stables and moved them out from under the dining room. Diners noticed the difference right away, especially during the humid Washington summers when the smell had ruined many an elegant meal. Among his other innovations was

piped-in water, still a rarity in most American homes in the 1830s. Water flowed through pipes from a spring some distance way, and collected into a pool from which it could be pumped into the kitchen. Although Jackson later added hot and cold running water, bathtubs, and even a shower, in the East Wing, water for bathing in the Residence itself had to be carried in buckets up two flights of stairs.

Inside the house, Jackson finally finished the East Room, which had been left in a raw state. Along with expensive wood paneling and cut glass chandeliers, twenty-four damask-covered armchairs and four matching sofas, the room's furnishings included twenty spittoons. In spite of his image as a roughshod backwoodsman, Jackson also had most of the interior repainted. The Green Room was still green, but he carefully chose a shade that would be more flattering to the ladies who gathered there.

Jackson reveled in entertaining, and added a third date to the official list of public parties. He had been responsible for winning the Battle of New Orleans that ended the recent war, and its date joined New Year's Day and the Fourth of July for public gatherings that were open to anyone who cared to drop by. Everyone was welcome, from government officials to their coachmen. Common laborers rubbed elbows with foreign ministers, and nobody liked that better than Andrew Jackson,

President Andrew Jackson

Among the personal effects of Andrew Jackson are (clockwise from top left): The Presidential Seal used for official documents. Made of copper-clad lead, it has a rosewood handle. The tag was written by President Rutherford B. Hayes; a top hat made by S.W. Handy of Washington. The wide mourning band is in honor of the President's late wife, Rachel; gold-framed spectacles with their case, made by John McAllister & Co., Philadelphia; a pearl and ruby stickpin; the President's pocketwatch, made by Hunter of Liverpool, England; a single-shot percussion pistol engraved with Jackson's name; a miniature oil portrait of Rachel on ivory. The President usually carried this with him wherever he went. She died a few months before he became president, and 10,000 people attended her funeral; and a hymnal, covered in needlepoint that belonged to Rachel.

who was proud to call himself the "People's President."

Near the end of his presidency, Jackson staged a party that easily topped his raucous inauguration day bash. Some of his admirers had sent him a 1,400-pound (635-kg) hunk of cheddar cheese, and on Washington's Birthday in 1837, less than two weeks before he moved back home to Tennessee, he invited the public into the house to have a taste. The City Marshall screened the guests at the door, but hundreds climbed in through the windows, creating the biggest crush of people the house had ever seen. The cheese was devoured in less than two hours, floors and carpets were ruined, and the smell of ripe cheese filled the mansion well into the administration of the next president, Martin Van Buren.

Van Buren had the common touch of his predecessor, but by contrast, his Executive Mansion didn't. While he was running for a second term (which he lost) in 1840, one of his opponent's supporters made one of the nastiest political speeches in the history of the Republic, forever remembered as the "Golden Spoon Speech."

ABOVE

Martin Van Buren discovered his flair for politics when he worked as a bartender in his father's tavern and learned the art of listening.

RIGHT

Van Buren's inauguration in the Senate chamber was overshadowed by the presence of this predecessor, Andrew Jackson, who was the only one to receive a standing ovation.

It was so extensive, it took the Congressman three days to unburden himself of it. Presented as a verbal tour of the house, it described a place with lavish banqueting halls, glittering saloons, and enough gold and silver to make the Russian Czar blush. The speechmaker reached a crescendo with a charge that the President, that very day, was dining on fine china with spoons made of solid gold.

Yes, indeed, Martin Van Buren had gold spoons. But he didn't have them bought. They were acquired by James Monroe, and every president since his day used them.

Van Buren's lifestyle was modest, in fact. But he was a bit of a dandy in the way he dressed and carried himself, and anyone who hadn't been inside the Executive Mansion could easily believe that the President slept in a bed "big as a barn door," and used dainty fingerbowls after meals of filet mignon. But the fact was, nearly everything in the house was there before he arrived. He didn't buy anything new, and as a tribute to his ancestry of thrifty Dutch farmers in the Hudson River Valley, he was careful to keep everything scrubbed and polished and in good repair.

Since, like his predecessors, Van Buren was expected to pay for entertainments at the Mansion, he chose not to have very many. He didn't open the house to the public until the New Year's Reception in 1838, when he had lived there for almost a year, and he canceled the Fourth of July party. And when the cheesemakers made him a gift of a giant wheel of cheddar, he had it placed in a local store where is was sold off for the benefit of a charity.

DEATH COMES TO THE HOUSE

The day William Henry Harrison became President, March 4, 1841, was the coldest inauguration day that anyone could remember. Yet the man delivered the longest inauguration speech anyone could remember. He wasn't wearing a coat and his hat was more often waving in the air at the end of his arm than on his head.

Exactly one month to the day later, President Harrison was dead after a series of ailments that began with a fever. He was the first resident of the House ever to have died there, and there was no precedent for funeral arrangements. His body lay in state in the darkened East Room, whose mirrors were

When William Henry Harrison ran for the presidency, he was presented as the hero of the battle of Tippecanoe against the Indians. Their slogan was "Tippecanoe and Tyler, too."

Born in Virginia in 1783, William Henry Harrison was the last president to have been born a British subject. He was sixty-eight at his inauguration.

When the Washington Monument was finished in 1884, it became the world's tallest masonry structure. But work had been halted for twenty-two years, prompting Mark Twain to say that it looked like "a factory chimney with the top broken off."

On his deathbed, Zachary Taylor, surrounded by his family and associates, including Jefferson Davis, the future president of the Confederacy, said, "I regret nothing, but I am sorry I am about to leave my friends."

draped in black, as was the exterior of the house.

On the morning of the funeral, the open coffin was moved to the entrance hall, and the public was allowed to pass by to pay their respects. Then it was moved back into the East Room for an invitation-only funeral. After the ceremony, it was placed on a special hearse drawn by eight white horses to the Congressional Cemetery. Just behind it in the procession was Harrison's own riderless horse.

Another riderless horse ambled down Pennsylvania Avenue less then ten years later. This time, the body on the hearse in front of it was the late President Zachary Taylor. He been the victim, apparently, not of the Washington winter, but of its brutal summer. On the Fourth of July in 1850, the President took part in ceremonies at the unfinished Washington Monument, and after a long day in the hot sun, he went home hungry and thirsty. Accounts vary on what he did about it, but it seems that he drank a huge amount of water, which came from a nearby well, and ate a large bowl-full of unwashed cherries with

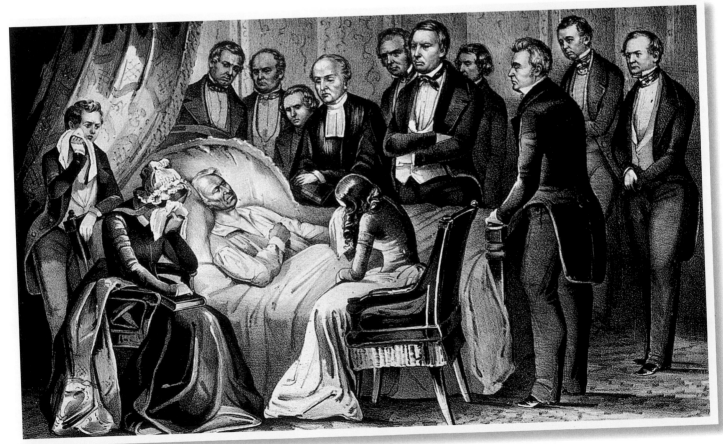

iced milk. A few hours later, he was complaining of stomach cramps. Five days later he was dead.

For this second funeral in the Mansion, the body also was placed in the East Room, but this time the public was allowed to file through. There were many floral tributes in the black-draped room, but before long there wasn't a petal or stem left. Souvenir-hunters walked off with everything.

The House went into mourning again in 1865 after the assassination of President Abraham Lincoln. As had now become a kind of tradition, his body lay in state in the East Room. And once again the public was allowed into the building to pay their respects. The doors officially opened at 9:30 in the morning, but long lines formed as early as 5:00. They entered through the black-draped north portico, then through the entrance hall to the Green Room and then into the darkened East Room.

The President's coffin was on a raised sixteen-foot (4.9-m) catafalque topped by a high black canopy. As before, all the mirrors, chandeliers, and furnishings were covered in black. As people approached, they were divided into two lines, and walked one-by-one past each side of the open coffin. None of them had waited less than six hours for the momentary glimpse they were allowed.

After the funeral, which was limited to 600—the capacity of the East Room—the coffin was placed on a funeral car pulled by six white horses. It was followed by Lincoln's own riderless horse, accompanied by a military escort, military bands, and representatives of the Union forces that had recently fought in the Civil War. There were some 30,000 marchers in the procession up Pennsylvania Avenue to the Capitol, and more than 100,000 watching them pass.

After lying in state in the Capitol Rotunda, the body was placed in a special railroad car for the trip back to the President's native Springfield, Illinois, for burial. The trip, which included stopovers in ten different cities, took twelve days.

BETTER DAYS

Although it couldn't save President Lincoln from death by assassination, there had been a security force in place at the Executive Mansion for almost twenty-five years by then. It had been instituted after a series of assassination threats to President John Tyler.

ABOVE

Deaths of presidents have always inspired special tributes, including new music such as the now forgotten National Funeral March written after Lincoln's assassination.

LEFT

When John Tyler married for the second time, he had eight children, and his second wife would present him with seven more. He was seventy when the last one was born.

BELOW

President James K. Polk and his wife, Sarah, never shied away from entertaining, but they did insist on having their parties alcohol-free.

BELOW RIGHT

At the time of his inauguration, Polk, at forty-nine, was the youngest president the country had seen.

The original force could hardly be called a force at all. It consisted of four unarmed men who doubled as doormen. They had the power to make arrests, but were encouraged not to, and confined their activities to giving the bum's rush to characters they considered suspicious. Most of the time, they served as presidential messengers.

Death came to the Tyler White House when the First Lady, Letitia, became the victim of a stroke in 1843. And that led to another first for the house, a presidential wedding. Less than a year after losing his wife, Tyler married Julia Gardiner, a woman half his age, whose family still holds an ancestral claim to the huge Gardiner's Island between the two eastern forks of Long Island.

In a bow to propriety, the wedding was held in New York rather than at the Executive Mansion, but as soon as they went home, Julia went to work bringing some life into the old house. Among other things, she introduced the waltz to Washington Society, and made it respectable for the first time. Then, for her next trick, she taught them how to polka. Her poor husband had been nervous about introducing his specialty, the Virginia reel, but soon that, too, became a staple at official balls and parties.

Tyler's successor, James Polk, accepted money from Congress to spruce up the Mansion, but vowed he would return half of it when his term ended. He was as good as his word. His contribution to presidential tradition was by ordering the Marine Band to play an old Scottish song called *Hail to the Chief* whenever he entered the room during official receptions. Polk was a small man who might have had a great career shadowing felons. He never stood out in a crowd. The martial music usually brought everyone to attention, even if they had a problem picking out the President from the crowd, and other marches served as a signal for them to quickstep to their assigned places at the tables. Other presidents who may not have needed the assist to assert their presence still follow his lead. And these days, any presidential affair without the Marine Band usually seems pretty somber.

The Polks introduced gas lighting to the house, but the President's wife, Sarah, used it sparingly. She much preferred candlelight.

Among James K. Polk's personal effects are (clockwise from top left):
A black satin damask smoking jacket tailored in a Turkish style. The jacket was given by James to his brother, Marshall, and then passed down through the family; a set of French porcelain costing $99.40, acquired by Alexander Stewart & Co., the first agent authorized to make purchases for the Executive Mansion. The service carries the Presidential Seal with 27 stars, representing the number of state in the Union in 1845; the Bible used by President Polk at his inauguration; an ivory-handled Presidential Seal; a gold-mounted cameo of the President owned by Sarah; dessert plates that were part of the presidential service. Polk was frugal, but turned the Mansion into a showplace. The china he had purchased was possibly the most elegant ever used in the house, before or since.

President Millard Fillmore, on the other hand, found such things as candles old-fashioned. He found the Executive Mansion a bit behind the times, too, and installed a modern heating system before he took on the kitchens. Even by the 1850s, the cooks were still working over open fireplaces, but Fillmore personally ordered a stove from a catalog intended for hotels. It came without an instruction book, and the President ordered drawings from the Patent Office so he could figure it out for himself. Then he personally staged a cook's tour of the contraption for the kitchen staff.

Fillmore had a strict rule that the house he lived in was "...a home of industry and temperance with plain diet, no tobacco, and no swearing," which must have put a crimp in the style of his fellow Washingtonians. But they would experience worse during the administration of Rutherford B. Hayes. One of them commented that "the water flowed like champagne" during his years there. Hayes also enforced a strict ban on "smoking and cussing," as well. Everybody said it was the work of his wife, who was known around town as "Lemonade Lucy."

ABOVE

When Oxford University offered Millard Fillmore an honorary degree, he refused to accept it, noting that it was written in Latin, and "no man should, in my judgment, accept a degree he cannot read."

RIGHT

Former First Ladies don't often host White House parties after they move on, but after Rutherford B. Hayes moved in, his predecessor's wife, Julia Grant, hosted one for him. It isn't know whether alcohol was served, but Hayes's wife, known as "Lemonade Lucy," didn't allow it at her own parties.

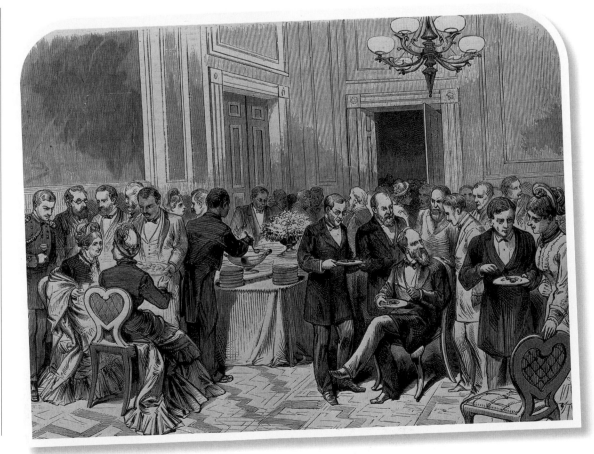

ONWARD AND UPWARD

Not long before Franklin Pierce was inaugurated, his only son Bennie, was killed in a train derailment which both he and his wife, Jane, survived. She was understandably devastated, and after moving into the Executive Mansion, she retired to an upstairs room, where she stayed, staring off into space, for nearly a year. All of the furniture in the house's public rooms was draped in black bunting.

As for the President, he turned to drink, and seemed to lose all interest in the job. But his drinking problem was curbed, and his interest was revived when work began on revitalizing the building they lived in. All of the state rooms on the main floor were redecorated and repairs were made to cracked walls and crumbling plaster. A bathroom with hot and cold running water was installed in the presidential living quarters for the first time, and a special screen was built to shield the north entrance from winter winds. The south grounds, which were still little more than a swamp, were upgraded and the greenhouses replaced by a conservatory where the President could get away from it all to sit in the sun surrounded by

exotic plants. The conservatory also proved to be a source of fresh flowers for the house itself, replacing the artificial flowers that had always been the standard.

When the work was completed, the Pierces opened their doors, and some 5,000 of their neighbors poured through the door to have a look at what had been accomplished. They also got their first look at Jane Pierce, who came downstairs for the first time to greet them.

Franklin Pierce's son died in an accident before he became president. Thinking it was God's punishment for his own sins, he refused to use a bible at his swearing-in. Instead, he swore allegiance to the U.S. Constitution.

During East Room receptions, President Pierce circled the room several times greeting his well-dressed guests. Drinking and dancing were forbidden, though. And card-playing was completely out of the question.

James Buchanan was the only American president who was never married. When a visitor mentioned that there was no lady in the house, he said, "That, madam, is my misfortune, not my fault."

People who had business with Pierce were shown to his office suite next to the family quarters. The inner sanctum consisted of an anteroom, a file room and secretary's office, and the presidential office itself, which doubled as a cabinet room.

The office contained a long table, a standup desk, a sofa, and some chairs. It left a lot to be desired, but it was more efficient that the arrangements previous presidents had made for themselves. Franklin Pierce was fascinated by the idea of efficiency.

So was his successor, James Buchanan, and he was just as interested in turning the Executive Mansion into a showplace. Our only bachelor president, he turned the details over to his niece, Harriet Lane, and she couldn't have been as enthusiastic about the job if she had actually been the First Lady. Official parties took on a new sparkle, and nobody ever turned down an invitation to one. She sold out-of-style furniture (some of which was repurchased and is back in the White House today), and had most of the rest recovered in brightly patterned fabrics. But it was all about to change once again.

After Abraham Lincoln moved in, his wife, Mary Todd Lincoln, went on a spending spree. Almost from the day she arrived, the house was

filled with workmen bringing the place up to her standards. Although she was generally frugal with her own money, she reveled in the idea of having government funds at her disposal. She took shopping trips to Philadelphia and New York regularly and often, and in less than nine months she spent all of the $20,000 that Congress had

Abraham Lincoln and his wife, Mary, had three sons, Tad, William, and Robert, the eldest, who was seventeen. Willie, the middle son, died at the age of ten in the White House.

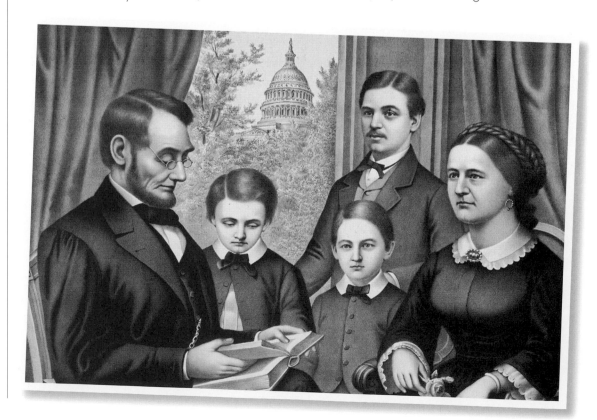

Among Abraham Lincoln's personal effects are (clockwise from top left): A Hariland-Limoges dessert plate from the presidential service; a tin poncet box that was to be found on Lincoln's desk; a brass call bell that was used to summon people to the president's office; a Swiss-made gold pocketwatch made from nuggets mined during the 1849 California Gold Rush and given to Lincoln by his friend, US Marshal Ward H. Lamon; an ebony cane with a silver cap that Lincoln carried on the night of his assassination at Ford's Theater and was later found in the box where he had been sitting; and a marble-topped mahogany table that was in Lincoln's Cabinet Room. He refused to allow hard liquor into his house, and this table was used to dispense ice water.

In the 1850s, foreign diplomatic delegations that visited Washington were sometimes Americans themselves. This group represented the Pawnee, Ponca, Potowatomi, and Chippewa who traveled from the West to meet the president.

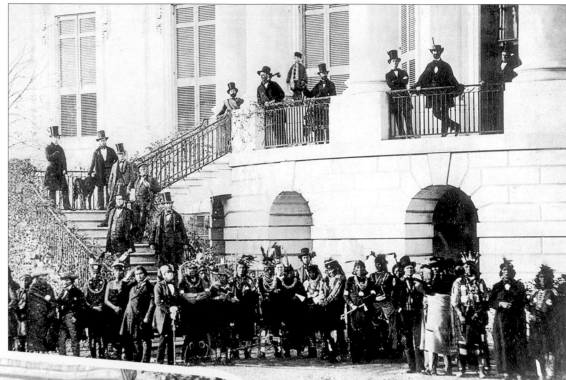

Abraham Lincoln was the first president to welcome blacks to his home as equals. Many of his predecessors brought them to the Executive Mansion as slaves.

appropriated for improvements, as well as $6,700 more.

When he was told of the oversight, Lincoln was furious. "It would stink to the nostrils of the American people to have it said that the President of the United States had approved a bill over-running an appropriation of $20,000 for flub-dubs for this damned old house," he thundered. He might have added the World War II chant, "Don't you know there's a war on?"

But Mary wasn't chastened. She also spent thousands on her wardrobe. "The people scrutinize every article that I wear," she said, "I must dress in costly material." She seemed especially fascinated by gloves. She seems to have bought 400 pairs in her first year as First Lady. In her defense, it should be pointed out that Mary Todd Lincoln was from a distinguished family, and presumably didn't have to depend entirely on her husband's meager salary as president.

Her most famous purchase was an ornate rosewood bed she bought for the state bedroom. The bed is eight feet (2.4m) long with an elaborate headboard and originally included a gilded canopy hung with satin and lace. President Lincoln himself never slept in it, although other presidents have. It was used by their son, Willie, who died in it at the age of ten of typhoid fever apparently contracted from the water that was piped into the house. It is now the centerpiece of the Lincoln Bedroom, which had formerly been President Lincoln's office.

PICKING UP THE PIECES

The Civil War took its toll on the Executive Mansion. Union troops had been billeted in the East Room, for one thing, leaving behind an infestation of lice, and there had been a steady

THE HOUSE AS A HOME

Grant, the daughter of President Ulysses S. Grant and his wife, Julia, was married there. The hapless bridegroom, a young Englishman, had the daunting job of asking the President of the United States for permission to marry his daughter, and Grant, who was opposed to the idea, was less than gracious.

But permission was granted, and as the spring wedding day approached in 1874, newspapers across the country began touting it as the most important social event of a generation. It may have been.

The East Room was filled to the ceiling with flowers, the bride wore a $2,000 wedding dress, and people climbed the trees around the house to catch a glimpse of her. Nellie and her husband went off to live in England, and were soon divorced, but the event put a spotlight on the Executive Mansion, and for the first time, newspapers and magazines started running endless stories about the house and the family that lived there. It was, and still is, the kind of attention usually lavished on royalty—the very thing the Founding Fathers had worked to avoid.

Andrew Johnson was a tailor before he became president and made all of his own clothes until he moved from Tennessee to his new home in Washington.

Although he objected to the match, President Ulysses S. Grant staged an elegant wedding for his only daughter, Nellie, when she married Algernon Sartoris in the Executive Mansion.

stream of important visitors, many of whom left with souvenirs in their pockets.

After Andrew Johnson moved in, the job of cleaning the place up fell to his wife, Eliza, and her daughters, Martha and Mary. In addition to battling rats and mice, they also scrubbed the place down from attic to cellar. They had Jefferson's old East Wing demolished and then had the West Wing rebuilt to accommodate a dairy.

When the Mansion was finally ready to receive guests, they made sure that all the carpets were covered and most of the furniture moved into rooms that could be locked. The woman also instituted new security measures. An official steward was hired, and made personally responsible for every bit of government property from spoons to settees. Because any losses would come from his own pocket, he managed to crimp the style of even the most creative souvenir-hunters.

The President himself was a baseball fan, and a diamond was built on the south grounds surrounded by a white picket fence. Other fans had to pay a quarter to watch games there.

A CHANGE OF LIFESTYLE

The average American was indifferent to the house their president called home until Nellie

The result was that Grant had to order all of the windows equipped with shutters that could be closed against prying eyes, and he declared the South Lawn off-limits to visitors so that the First Family could get some privacy out-of-doors.

Although the Grants added a lot of furniture and made some improvements to the house during their eight years there, not much was done beyond basic upkeep until Chester A. Arthur arrived on the scene. It was not for nothing that newspapers called him "Elegant Arthur," and when he took a look at the house, he declared it "a badly kept barracks," and refused to move in. He personally inspected every room and put labels on things he couldn't live with. In all, twenty-four wagon-loads of the accumulation of years were hauled away to be auctioned off.

During the renovations that followed, the Army Corps of Engineers inspected the Mansion and declared that it would be an act of mercy to demolish it and start over. But thanks to public pressure and congressional disapproval, it was decided to fix the old place up instead.

Arthur then commissioned no less a person than Louis Comfort Tiffany to redecorate it.

Among the Tiffany touches were bronze and copper stars on the ceiling of the Red Room, which was repainted in a color close to maroon. The Blue Room became robin's-egg blue with the top half of the walls papered in ivory. The most talked-about design detail was a stained glass screen that replaced the one that had been installed to keep wind from blowing through the north-facing door. It was fifty feet (15.2m) long and ten feet (3m) high, and it sparkled with red, white, and blue jewels.

The widowed Grover Cleveland married the former Frances Folsom in the Blue Room in 1886, and although the ceremony was private, they were hounded by reporters as they honeymooned in western Maryland. When they returned home, the President cautioned his wife that the job of being First Lady would be much easier if she didn't try anything new. And kept away from reporters. She wasn't able to take his advice on the latter, and she wasn't inclined to pay any attention to the former. Frances was

Grover Cleveland was a workaholic. He even worked on his wedding day which, conveniently, took place in the Blue Room. He personally oversaw every tiny detail in the running of the household as though it were a matter of national security.

William McKinley's wife, Ida, suffered from epilepsy, but the word was never used. She was said to be "delicate." Ida outlived the president, and was at his side when he was assassinated in 1901.

the youngest of all her predecessors, and she loved entertaining. At her first reception, she and her husband were obliged to shake the hands of some 9,000 well-wishers.

The dogged attention of the press, and Cleveland's determination to keep the house open to the people, made receptions like that one the norm. During Benjamin Harrison's administration, the floors of the State Rooms were reinforced to handle the weight of the crowds that gathered there, and a wooden bridge was built leading from a window in the East Room to allow more people to enter and leave the building at the same time.

Things got worse when William McKinley lived there. Government engineers warned him that the weight of 2,000 people was the limit the house could stand, but his parties more often than not attracted half again as many. It wasn't that he invited all those people, though. Sometimes an invited guest would bring along a friend or two, but the big problem was with the uninvited guests. The gatekeeper complained that he was being inundated by "butchers, market and grocery clerks, the scum of the city." There wasn't much he could do about it, though, except to enforce a rule of his own making, that men wouldn't be admitted if they weren't dressed in evening clothes. It helped a little.

3 A New Century

The house, nor Washington itself, had never seen anything quite like the family of President Theodore Roosevelt. Among the first changes his wife, Edith, instituted was to have a tennis court installed, and her husband played close to 100 games a day. He might have played more of them if he could have found an opponent he hadn't already worn out.

RIGHT

In Theodore Roosevelt's day, the Cabinet met in an office building overlooking the White House tennis court.

FAR RIGHT

It's a bird! No, it's a plane. And it's not stuck on the White House roof. It is a Wright Type B, piloted by Harry Atwood, taking off from the lawn in 1911.

When he had time to spare, Roosevelt practiced jujitsu and boxing, took long horseback rides, and went off on four- or five-mile (6.4- or 8-km) runs. In spite of his presidential workload that kept four typists and six stenographers exhausted, he was unusually attentive to his six children, ranging in age from seventeen to four.

His eldest child, Alice, who lived on to become a doyen of Washington Society, seemed to be the ringleader of this gang of mischief-makers. She had a pet garter snake named Emily Spinach that she carried in her handbag waiting for opportunities to let it out in the company of guests she knew would be shocked, or frightened, or both. She loved to take the others sledding on serving trays down the Grand Stairway, and when her father told her in no uncertain terms that he wouldn't allow her to smoke under his roof, she found her way to the roof and went up there to enjoy an occasional cigarette. When it snowed, her brothers and sister would go up there to throw snowballs at people passing by.

Among other ways the youngsters found to amuse themselves was to follow the lamplighter around the grounds, turning off each light as soon as he went on to the next one. They also enjoyed stilt-walking through the flower beds, and roller skating through the hallways. At one point they even managed to smuggle a pony into the elevator. Just before they moved out,

The Roosevelt family was rarely this still. From left to right, they are: Quentin, President Roosevelt, Ted, Archie, Alice, Kermit, First Lady, Edith, and Ethel.

the President wrote in a letter to his son, Kermit, that, "I don't think that any family has ever enjoyed the White House more than we have."

Although few people would have taken any bets on it, Alice finally grew up, and in 1906, she married Congressman Nicholas Longworth in what was possibly the most elaborate White House wedding before or since. Huge crowds gathered outside, and more than a thousand crammed into the East Room for the ceremony, which produced reams of copy for nearly every newspaper in the country, most of which called her "Princess Alice."

The previous concerns about overcrowding in the house had virtually vanished by then. The Roosevelts moved out to their home in Oyster Bay, New York, less than a year after they moved in, and work began rebuilding the White House. Most of the furniture, including the famous Tiffany glass screen at the door, was hauled off and sold at auction (the screen fetched $275).

Charles McKim, of the firm McKim, Mead & White, was hired to replace the stuff and to redecorate the interior. He concluded that the interior would need to be completely overhauled, but the President insisted that the changes should be sensitive to the past. "The White House is the property of the nation," he wrote, "and so far as it is compatible with living therein should be kept as it originally was."

"Living therein" was a big concern. He and his wife and their six children were crammed into the eight-room family quarters. The style of his official life was cramped as well, and it had become standard procedure to seat dinner guests in the hallway outside the State Dining Room.

The official offices upstairs had reached a bursting point, and McKim moved them out into a new extension of the West Wing, which also freed up more space for the family quarters on the second floor. The wing itself was set back from the front of the mansion, and at the bottom of a slope, which made it completely unobtrusive.

He also moved the public entrance into the East Wing, which, like its mate, extended out 160 feet (48.8m) from the main house. He fitted it out with coat rooms and rest rooms for the convenience of arriving guests. The north entry, which had always been the main one, became a private entrance. Edith clashed with the architect over the removal of the

greenhouses that had been the main feature of both the East and West Wings that Thomas Jefferson had envisioned as service areas, but McKim prevailed by suggesting building new, modern conservatories elsewhere.

He enlarged the State Dining Room by replacing a load-bearing wall with a steel truss and relocating the Grand Stairway. Among his other improvements was the restoration of the

The East Room was gorgeously decorated in anticipation of Alice Roosevelt's wedding in 1906. It was one of the most lavish weddings ever held at the White House.

Theodore Roosevelt gave Alice's hand in marriage to Congressman Nicholas Longworth, Washington's most sought-after bachelor. Her mother said, "I'm glad to see you go. You've never been anything but trouble."

RIGHT

President Taft's Cabinet was an impressive collection of men, but he was much happier with the company he kept after his presidency when he became a Justice of the Supreme Court.

BELOW

Taft seemed born to be a politician. But charisma still needs to be backed by campaign buttons. The other guy is vice presidential candidate, James S. Sherman.

basement hall and adding of new kitchens. The old furnace room became the Diplomatic Reception Room.

The new offices in the West Wing included two secretary's offices, a room for the stenographers' pool, a press room, and a telegraph room. File rooms and closets were placed in the basement under the wing. The President's office (the Oval Office would come later) was a rather plain room, especially considering Roosevelt's colorful personality, about thirty feet square.

In the public rooms, McKim carefully worked for simplicity. The floors were bleached and waxed, painted surfaces were sanded to a high gloss, and all the rooms were finished in their traditional colors. Most of the furniture was reproductions of antiques. It could easily have passed for the home of any of the previous presidents, except for the occasional moosehead staring down on visitors.

Up to this point, the house had always reflected the lifestyle, and the style of the day, of the families that lived there. Now, for the first time, it had been transformed into a place that had historical references to all of them. It had become a kind of stage set for the drama of the presidency in a brand-new century.

REARRANGING THE STAGE

By the time William Howard Taft filled Teddy Roosevelt's shoes, the decoration of the house seemed to have gone about as far as it could go. But Nellie Taft, the new First Lady, wasn't without ideas. For her first trick, she replaced the white ushers with black men, and dressed them in blue livery, designating some of them as footmen, who she decreed should be at the door at all hours. Next, she sent down an order that all men on the staff must be clean-shaven. Then she fired the man who had served as steward during the Roosevelt years, not because he wouldn't shave, but because she believed the job ought to be held by a woman.

Frustrated by the fact that there wasn't much she could do to change the downstairs decor, Nellie took on the family quarters upstairs, filling it with oriental pieces and colorful fabrics. She also had a grand piano made for herself and installed it in a sitting room she carved out of one of the wide corridors. She carried her love for oriental flavors out into the city itself by creating a new public park, which she had planted with 2,000 Japanese cherry trees, donated by the Mayor of Tokyo.

Her husband, meanwhile, made some changes in the West Wing, installing the first

Oval Office. It may have been simply because he needed more space. The President weighed 350 pounds (159kg). He had to have a special seven-foot-long (2.1-m) bathtub made. It was forty-one inches (104cm) wide and it weighed almost a ton.

Woodrow Wilson's first wife, Ellen, who died in the White House a year after they moved in, also concentrated on enhancing the family quarters, including expanding them to the former attic above. She also replaced Edith Roosevelt's colonial garden on the west side of the mansion with a more formal Italianate rose garden.

The President married the former Edith Bolling Galt not long afterward, at her home, not his. Although she lived there for six years, she didn't make many cosmetic changes, but during those years, the life of the White House was altered dramatically. In order to save money and manpower at the beginning of World War I, Wilson turned a flock of sheep loose to keep the lawns clipped. The flock grew, as sheepflocks will, and the "White House Wool" was sold, raising more than $100,000 to support the troops in France.

LEFT

Although Taft really didn't want to be president, his wife, Helen, also known as "Nellie," loved being First Lady.

BELOW

In 1918, President Wilson put a herd of sheep to work clipping the White House lawn. Not only were they quieter than lawnmowers, but also their wool was sold to help support the war effort.

Woodrow Wilson was the best educated of all the presidents. He earned a PhD at Johns Hopkins University, and served as President of Princeton University.

President Warren G. Harding, and his wife, "Flossie," regularly greeted people from the White House porch. He ran his presidential campaign from his front porch back in Marion, Ohio.

The war took a personal toll on the President, and he eventually suffered an apparent stroke, which some said had caused brain damage. Although it was officially characterized as a "digestive upset," the man was almost totally incapacitated for seven months, his left arm and leg paralyzed. The house had been closed to visitors during the war, and it was shut down once again as the First Lady assumed the day-to-day running of the presidency behind closed doors. As his health began to improve, and he was seen on the porch in a wheelchair, there was talk that he would resign, but he not only refused to consider the idea, but announced plans to run for a third term.

RETURN TO NORMALCY

By the time the Wilson presidency ended, the Roaring Twenties had breezed in, and the new President, Warren G. Harding, whose campaign had been based on a call for a "Return to Normalcy," brought a new era to the White House. After having been virtually boarded up for past three years, the lights blazed inside again, and the public was invited too. When the new First Lady, Florence Harding, who her husband called "The Dutchess," found the servants instinctively drawing the curtains over the windows, she said, "Let 'em look in if they want to. It's their White House."

And they came by the thousands. The gates were left open, and anybody who wanted to walk in was free to go just about anywhere they wanted to. Few rooms were off-limits. Harding himself routinely appeared around lunchtime each day to shake hands with visitors, and his wife frequently gave them personal tours of the place.

The Hardings were also enthusiastic entertainers, often inviting guests into their private quarters upstairs. The long-abandoned custom of New Year's receptions and Fourth of July parties were brought back, and they introduced Easter-egg rolling to the White House lawn, as well as garden parties for the adults.

The Eighteenth Amendment to the Constitution had made drinking illegal anywhere, and the White House was, naturally, dry at the time. But the President, who himself was allergic to alcohol, regularly entertained his hard-drinking political cronies (many of whom, like he

Among President Wilson's personal effects are (clockwise from top left): A gold medal, presented by the King of Belgium (his head adorns the coin), with a leather presentation case embossed with the Great Seal of the United States; a silver and gilt "peace casket" presented by the City of London; the President's white detachable collar; a gold-headed cane; a silk top hat; white dress gloves; a pair of gold stickpins embossed with the Presidential Seal; a leather jewelry box, adorned with the President's initials in gold; a California gold nugget intended to be made into a wedding band for the Wilsons; a medal awarded by the City of Verdun, France; rimless gold wire spectacles; a gold watch fob; a cigarette lighter—a gift from French Premiere Georges Clemenceaux; and the pen Wilson used to sign the declaration of war against Germany in 1917.

President Calvin Coolidge and his wife, Grace, keeping cool with a bit of ice cream at a White House garden party. The First Lady sometimes did her own cooking at the White House.

On Christmas Eve, 1929, a major fire almost completely destroyed the West Wing. President Hoover's sons joined the hundred firefighters to limit the damage.

himself, had supported the amendment) and managed to secure a license to buy hooch "for medical purposes." The "boys" were usually entertained in the President's bedroom, where "we can do as we like."

After Harding died, and was replaced by his Vice President, Calvin Coolidge, everything changed again. Coolidge was a man of simple habits and few words. When it was announced that he had died, Dorothy Parker said, "How could they tell?"

But if he didn't talk much, "Silent Cal" invented the White House press conference, and showed up twice a week to answer reporters' questions. He insisted, though, that the questions should be submitted in advance, and after reading them over, he frequently announced that none of them interested him, and that the press conference was over.

Grace Coolidge seemed to be her husband's direct opposite. She loved giving lavish parties for important guests, and for the first time movie stars were made to feel welcome in the State Dining Room. The President kept her on a short leash, though, forbidding her to dance in public or to have her hair bobbed, as nearly every other woman in America was doing. But he encouraged her to buy the best and latest fashions. It was said that she spent $5,000 a week on her

wardrobe, and never appeared at White House functions wearing the same gown twice.

Grace was also the first First Lady to ask the public to donate antique furniture to the White House rather than to museums. But the President let her know in no uncertain terms that he wouldn't allow any redecorating of the house itself. There was, however, one job he had no control over. The roof over the family quarters had begun to sag, and engineers concluded that it needed to be totally replaced. In the process, they added eighteen more rooms, including two guest rooms and several bathrooms, plus new closets for Grace's growing collection of dresses. A skylight brightened the central corridor, and a new solarium that opened onto a tiled patio created a bright presidential retreat above the maddening crowd.

GETTING THROUGH HARD TIMES

As if the 1929 Stock Market crash hadn't brought enough misery to President Herbert Hoover, on Christmas Eve that year, fire destroyed the West Wing. By morning, only the brick walls were left on the north side and although there was less damage to the south, it, too, was little more than a charred shell.

The wing had become cramped by then, and the fire seemed to present an opportunity for a badly needed expansion. But in the midst

either in a wheelchair or aided by heavy leg braces. It required the building of special ramps throughout the house, but that was only part of the change that would come during his twelve years there, the longest of any of the presidents.

During the late years of the Depression and into World War II, FDR delivered what he called "fireside chats" to the American people. There was no television then, and the chats were broadcast on the radio, but when he discovered that the fireplace in the Diplomatic Reception Room, where he gave the talks, wasn't a real one, he had it ripped out and replaced with one that worked. As was the case with nearly every president, FDR's staff was far larger than his predecessors, and he was forced to double the amount of office space in the West Wing. But rather than expanding outward, he had the space under it excavated. Then he reconfigured the space on the ground floor, moving the Oval Office over to the southeast corner. At the same time, a

Herbert Hoover was a mining millionaire. He donated his salary to charity. He never carried any money, and usually borrowed what he needed from whoever might be handy.

President Franklin D. Roosevelt had been an Assistant Secretary of the Navy, and an avid yachtsman. His taste in decorating leaned to ships and seascapes.

of the Great Depression, Hoover opted to have it rebuilt almost exactly as it had been. The abundance of available labor in the early Depression years made it possible to rebuild the whole wing in less than a year.

Meanwhile, the Hoovers kept up appearances with an almost endless round of luncheons, receptions, and formal dinners. About a thousand people were invited to the White House every day, and on many days, twice as many showed up. About the only times the President wasn't pleased to see White House visitors was when 15,000 World War I veterans camped along the Anacostia River and marched on the White House demanding a bonus that had been promised to them.

Hoover wouldn't meet with them, but ordered they be treated with dignity. General Douglas MacArthur, who commanded the Army in Washington back then, ignored the order and burned down the veteran's camp after running them off with tanks and bayonet-wielding troops. It wouldn't be the last time the General thumbed his nose at his Commander-in-Chief.

A NEW DEAL

After suffering from poliomyelitis, President Franklin D. Roosevelt wasn't able to walk, but he managed to get around the White House

The White House swimming pool was a godsend to FDR; as a wheelchair-bound victim of polio he couldn't exercise any other way than by swimming.

ABOVE

Campaign buttons are at the heart of every presidential campaign. FDR won four of them, but now the Constitution forbids anyone to run more than twice.

RIGHT

Truman was surprised when FDR chose him as his running mate in 1944. After the President died, everyone was surprised at how well Truman filled his shoes.

swimming pool was built for the President in the basement space between the house and the wing.

As even more people came to work at the White House during the war years, the East Wing was demolished and a new one built with its first floor reserved for the White House police and general office space on the floor above. Beneath it, in a subbasement, was a secret bomb shelter, just in case the shooting war came to Washington.

At about the same time, First Lady Eleanor Roosevelt also had the basement kitchen modernized. It became big enough, and efficient enough, to prepare 7,000 full course meals in a day. The White House cook was pleased to report that she baked forty loaves of bread and two dozen pies at the same time, while a covey of quail was roasting in the broiler. Part of the reconstruction of the kitchen area eliminated an old storeroom that was turned into the Library. The second-floor Oval Room that had been used as a library for a half-century, was transformed into a sitting room.

In a time of food rationing and world-wide starvation, Mrs. Roosevelt made it a point to serve simple food—it was said that she considered eating a poor second to rich conversation at luncheons and dinner parties—and made it a point to let America know that the President himself often ate leftovers. And liked it.

The First Lady had a huge following of admirers, and in addition to answering upwards of 300,000 letters a year, she also

wrote magazine articles and books, lectured extensively, and wrote a weekly syndicated newspaper column. It all brought in a tidy income that was larger than her husband's.

She also ran the household, and catered to hundreds of important guests. Among them was British Prime Minister Winston Churchill, who came several times for extended stays in the early Forties. But the most memorable White House guests of the Roosevelts was King George VI and Queen Elizabeth of Britain, who stayed there for one memorable night in 1939. It was the first time any British ruler had ever visited America.

DOWN WITH THE OLD

When Franklin D. Roosevelt died, his Vice President, Harry S. Truman, said to some reporters, "Boys if you ever pray, pray for me now." He might also have added, "Pray for the White House, too."

When his wife, Bess, was given her first tour of the place, she declared that it reminded her of an abandoned hotel. Her twenty-one year-old daughter, Margaret, said that it depressed her. As for himself, the President was convinced that the place must be haunted. There were all sort of strange noises in the night that might have been caused by the shades of all the strong-willed people who had lived there. But it actually was wind blowing through wide cracks, floors groaning under the weight of heavy furniture, and other sad sounds of a house that was itself at death's door.

Among President Harry S. Truman's personal effects are (clockwise, from top left): A gray felt borsalino hat with a black silk band; a silk pattened sport shirt which, like the hat, was a Truman trademark; a movie camera given to the President by newsreel photographers; a white twill and mesh cap that Truman wore on his many visits to Key West, Florida; aviator-style sunglasses; a pair of white and tan spectator shoes; a gold-headed walking stick; a cane with the Democratic donkey as its handle; a wooden gavel used to open the 79th Congress; a nickel-cased pocketwatch; a gold jewel of a Scottish Rite Master Mason; a Thirty-Third Degree Masonic ring; a Thirty-Second Degree Master Mason ring; a gold jewel of the Knights Templar; a Masonic apron made for Truman as Grand Master of Freemasons in Missouri; a pair of eyeglasses; and a pair of brown leather gloves.

The BUCK STOPS here!

Fed up with how the bureaucracy "passed the buck" of responsibility to others, Truman had this wood and glass sign made for his desk.

Truman was a self-confessed "architectural nut," and one of his first priorities was to get rid of the awnings that had been stretched between the columns of the South Portico. It would be much nicer, he thought, if there was a balcony above it to provide the needed shade. But he had no sooner commissioned an architect to design one when he was told that any such change would need the permission of the Fine Arts Commission. "The hell with them," he shot back, "I'm going to do it anyway." The awnings came down, and the balcony went up. But it turned out to be too public for the family actually to use. As it turned out, Harry Truman's first experience with architects and builders was just the overture.

Margaret Truman was hoping to become—and her father was—a pretty fair piano player, so it was only natural that they would have a piano upstairs in their quarters. But when it was

put into place, one of its legs broke through the floor. The President had noticed that the chandelier in the East Room swayed back and forth when the color guard marched through. And he said that he always felt the floor shake upstairs whenever "that big fat butler brought me my breakfast." The last straw came when he was taking a bath upstairs and felt the floor giving way under him; he had a vision of himself floating down into the midst of some reception or other going on below.

That was when he ordered a thorough inspection of the house. The verdict was that the house was falling down. The only really safe spot in the whole building, the engineers reported, was the so-called "Truman Balcony." As Truman explained it, the White House was standing "purely out of habit."

The President was immediately moved to a lower floor for his own safety, and a few days later, he and his family were moved across the street to Blair House. That was in 1948; they wouldn't be able to move back until 1952. Truman was driven back across the street every day to go to work in the West Wing, which had only recently been rebuilt itself. It kept him close to the action and, as an "architectural nut," he had a problem keeping his mind on the business of state.

During those four years, the White House was completely gutted and the interior totally rebuilt. One of the most serious problems was the old timbers that had been put in place during the 1817 rebuilding couldn't support the weight of the structure any longer. Not to mention that they had dried out and represented a serious fire hazard. All of the water pipes, electrical wiring, and air ducts that had been added since then were not only cut through beams and bearing walls, but added more weight for them to bear.

During the 1902 restoration, one of those bearing walls was taken away to make the State Dining Room bigger, and although steel

First Lady Bess Truman and her daughter, Margaret, found themselves exiled to Blair House across the street while the White House was being reconstructed.

Construction supervisors on the White House lawn during its 1950 reconstruction never knew when the President himself might join them with a little advice.

During the Truman reconstruction, only the outside walls of the White House were left standing. The inside became a jungle of steel girders and reinforcing braces.

beams had been inserted under the State Floor, they rested on old stone and brick walls that shifted under their weight. Finally, when the steel-and-concrete addition was made to the third floor, in 1927, it added an almost intolerable burden to the supports below it.

Truman was given several options to solve the problem, including tearing the place down and starting over. He chose the most difficult option: to save the walls, the third floor, and the roof and tear out the rest. If Harry Truman loved architecture, he was also crazy about history. "I'll do anything in my power to keep them from tearing down the White House," he said.

Congress went along with him and appropriated $5.4 million to do the job. Work began on December 12, 1949. It started with digging a series of pits through the clay down to a solid section of gravel and sand about twenty-five feet (7.6m) down. Concrete was poured into them to form footings for the walls, which would soon have to support more weight than ever. At the same time, work began on dismantling the interior. Most of the woodwork was cracked and dry and not easily recycled, and it was hauled away. Plaster casts were made of old moldings and cornices so that they could be reproduced.

Steel beams were put in place for stability, and then the interior walls were removed. At the same time, a permanent steel skeleton was put in place to support the building as it never had been before. Within a few months, nothing of the original building was left inside.

As work continued, all of the old rooms began to reemerge. But this time, their floors were concrete (they would be covered with wood flooring), and air ducts, plumbing, and electrical systems were installed inside the walls without changing their original dimensions. Before long, interior designers were at work restoring the colors, the mantels, the woodwork, and everything else in all the rooms to their original colors and decor. As their final act, they repainted the exterior. White, of course.

RESTORATION

While the White House was being rebuilt, most of the furnishings were stored by the New York department store, B. Altman. Its design director was appointed to oversee the refurbishing of the rooms, and also to repair and refurbish the things that were in their warehouse.

The cost of rebuilding made buying antiques out of the question, and it was decided to concentrate on reproductions of late nineteenth-century neoclassical furnishings. Truman also received gifts of paintings and other antique artifacts from foreign heads of state. But, compared to their former appearance, the rooms seemed a bit empty and without the reflections of the personalities of previous presidents that had added to the White House's charm (or clutter, as many had charged).

After Dwight D. Eisenhower and his wife, Mamie, moved in, little was changed except, of course, in the private quarters, but the First Lady added immensely to the china collection through donations from the families of previous presidents. She also accepted a bequest from the late Margaret Thompson Biddle of more than 1,500 pieces of gilded silver, and designated a special ground-floor room to display the priceless collection.

When John F. Kennedy and his wife, Jacqueline, arrived at the White House, they were appalled at what they found. She called it "the dreary Maison Blanche."

Even before the inauguration, Jackie was making plans to turn the White House into "a showcase of American arts and history," and her first act as First Lady was to form a Fine Arts Commission to do the job. Their mandate was to locate furnishings and art, and convince their owners to donate them, as well as cash

Before moving into the White House, former General Dwight D. Eisenhower and his wife, Mamie, had changed addresses an average of once a year throughout their marriage.

Among the personal effects of President Dwight D. Eisenhower are (clockwise from top left): A Bible (American Standard Version) given to him by his mother when he graduated from West Point in June 1915. He only graduated with average grades. The front of it is embossed with the words "Dwight D. Eisenhower" and he went on to use it in his presidential inauguration; the black homberg hat with grain ribbon that he wore at his inauguration. The interior label identifies the retailer as F.R. Tripler & Co., Madison Avenue at 46th Street; a white silk scarf with the Declaration of Independence and the Great Seal screened on it; a pair of gray, fine-grained leather gloves worn by Eisenhower; Mrs. Eisenhower's evening gloves; the First Lady's beaded evening bag; and the program for one of many inaugural balls held in the President's honor.

President John F. Kennedy's two children, JFK, Jr., known as John-John, and Caroline, were possibly the most-photographed youngsters in America in the early sixties.

First Lady Jacqueline Kennedy (left) wasn't happy with the decorative legacy her predecessors had left her, and redecorated all of the White House.

donations to improve the settings they would be displayed in. She also set up the Office of the Curator, and established the White House Historical Association. In other words, she turned the White House into a museum. Later, she lobbied for legislation that made the contents of the house the property of the people and not the incumbent president.

Her campaign for donations, culminated by a televised tour of the house in 1962 that reached an audience of forty-two million, resulted in the acquisition of more than 1,100 historical antiques and works of art. Congress, as it had done for previous presidents, appropriated $50,000 for redecorating, but Jackie went through that in less than two weeks. For everything else, she had to rely on the generosity of private donors.

Although the Kennedy project was an all-American enterprise, Jackie hired a French designer, Stéphane Boudin, who had redecorated Malmaison, the former home of Josephine Bonaparte near Paris. He advised her on color schemes, draperies, and the arrangements of the furniture and painting as well as the lighting. Nearly all of the rooms had been changed at one time or another during the administrations of successive presidents, and so they didn't feel bound to the specific history of any particular period. They tried, though, to recreate the mood of the early nineteenth century, especially in the parlors. Boudin's French touch is most striking in the Blue Room, which had been furnished in a French Empire style by James Madison, and was redecorated in the style during the 1902 restoration. He also re-introduced a classical style to the Red Room, reflecting a Classical style popular in the early nineteenth century. It became popular again, thanks to him, and historic houses restored during the 1960s nearly all had rooms that looked strangely like the Red Room at the White House.

In less than three years, nearly every public room, and most of the private ones, had been completely redone and refurnished. Today, almost forty years later, most Americans believe that nothing has changed since 1963. Of course, that isn't quite the case. But it has changed less than during any other period in its history.

requested the conversion of the Map Room into a sitting room with Chippendale furniture made in the eighteenth century. On the other side of the coin, he also had a bowling alley installed under the driveway.

Hundreds of rare antiques were added to the White House collection during the Nixon years, but he may be best remembered around the house for his attempt to change the appearance of the White House police. Calling them "slovenly," he ordered new uniforms designed for them, and they appeared one morning dressed in costumes that might have been more appropriate for a Viennese operetta—pillbox hats, white tunics, and heavy draping of gold braid. Visitors couldn't help smirking, and the press jumped all over the new look. In a couple of days, the uniforms were packed away in mothballs, and the police resumed their original slovenly appearance, although spit and polish became the order of the day.

Two years into the administration of Gerald R. Ford, the country celebrated the first 200 years of its history, and he and his wife entertained an unprecedented number of foreign dignitaries at the White House. The event also prompted a large number of Americans to donate money, as well as historic furnishings for its enhancement. As for herself, Betty Ford, like Eleanor Roosevelt before her, was especially interested in American crafts, and borrowed examples of it from the Smithsonian Institution to use as centerpieces for state dinners, and as decorative elements in many of the rooms.

LEFT

President Lyndon B. Johnson's wife was named Claudia, but she was much better-known as "Lady Bird," or, as the President preferred, just plain "Bird."

BELOW LEFT

Oddly, there had never been a fashion show at the White House until Lady Bird Johnson staged one in 1968 for the wives of 43 governors attending a conference there.

BELOW

Richard Nixon's family included (L-R) David Eisenhower, grandson of the former president, Julie Eisenhower, the current president's daughter, President Nixon, First Lady Pat Nixon, and daughter Patricia.

. A good deal of the credit for that goes to President Lyndon B. Johnson, who formed the Committee for the Preservation of the White House. He also made the position of White House Curator a permanent one.

As for themselves, the Johnsons made almost no changes in the White House while they lived there. But when President Richard Nixon and his wife, Pat, moved there in 1969, the house was beginning to show signs of wear. The Kennedy restoration had excited most Americans and they were flocking there by the thousands to take a look at their house.

The new First Lady and the Preservation Commission changed several rooms, especially the Green Room and the Red Room, and began an intensive campaign to acquire early nineteenth-century decorative arts. The President

Sometimes a First Lady has to get her hands dirty, as Rosalynn Carter found out when she planted some new trees outside the White House.

In 1983, President Ronald Reagan and First Lady, Nancy, hung ornaments on the White House Christmas tree made for them by two Korean children they had brought back on Air Force One *for heart surgery.*

Jimmy Carter and his wife, Rosalynn, were less interested in putting their personal stamp on the White House than almost any other presidential couple before them. They were fascinated by the historical aspects of their new home, and the First Lady scoured store rooms, as Jackie Kennedy had before her, for historical furnishings. Amazingly, there were quite a few that had been overlooked, and they were brought out to where they could be seen. Rosalynn was also instrumental in the acquisition of several important paintings.

Most importantly, Mrs. Carter established the private non-profit White House Preservation Fund, which set up an endowment and relieved the Preservation Committee from the job of begging for money for specific projects.

While presidents before him often went around turning off lights to cut down on the electric bill, Carter went on a veritable cost-cutting binge. Among the things he discovered in his search for waste were 325 television sets in the West Wing and the White House, as well as 220 radios. Most of them went, but it's a good bet that new ones replaced them and the number by now is much, much higher than that. How else could the staff have kept up with the next president, Ronald Reagan, well-known as the "Great Communicator"?

When Reagan communicated with the press, it was always in the East Room, where he stood in front of the open doors so that the television cameras could capture the full grandeur of the occasion. As former actors, both he and his wife, Nancy, knew the value of the dramatic possibilities the White House offered and hardly ever missed a chance to present the public with a picture of great pomp and tradition.

During their residency, the mansion achieved a kind of formality to the place that belied the First Family's laid-back California lifestyle. During those eight years in the White House, the Reagans entertained seven kings, three queens, thirteen princes, seventy-seven prime ministers, forty-five foreign ministers, and one sheik. The 75,700-piece china set they used cost almost $210,000, donated by a private foundation.

The First Lady called herself a "frustrated decorator," and set about redecorating the private quarters and well as some of the rooms downstairs. In all, she spent more than a million dollars on improvements, restoration, and repairs. Yet when the usual $50,000 earmarked for such things arrived from Congress, she sent it back, and issued a call for private donations to give her some *real* money to work with. She never had to ask anyone twice.

George H.W. Bush reported that "the house has never been in better shape," when his family moved in. His wife, Barbara, seemed relieved to add, "I don't have to think about decorating or improvements." Of course, there is always something that needs tending to when a new tenant arrives. Among other changes, she converted the Reagan gym into a suite of guest rooms for her family, which included five grown children and thirteen grandchildren. The Reagans had commandeered some of the former bedrooms to use as office space, and when the Bushes moved in, the White House had only nine bedrooms.

After Bill Clinton's inauguration, First Lady Hillary Rodham Clinton took on the traditional role of taking charge of the White House's furnishings and decorations, by sprucing up the Blue Room. Among the changes was altering the color to a sapphire blue, chosen without apology for its ability to look good under harsh television lighting.

The house had always been a kind of museum, even before it formally became one after the Kennedy restoration, but it is a museum where people have been encouraged to walk through the rooms as if it were their own home. The Clintons were especially sensitive to the idea of keeping it that way and making it, if anything, more accessible to more people.

They were also sensitive to the care of the house itself, and even before work began on the Blue Room, the exterior was stripped of forty coats of paint and the stone facade repaired. The next refurbishing project took place in the State Dining Room, where some 60,000 guests assemble every year. Then the Cross Hall outside the East Room was recarpeted, once again with an eye on how it would look on television. Mrs. Clinton next had the Map Room redecorated, bringing it as close to the way it looked when President Franklin Roosevelt and British Prime Minister Winston Churchill met there so often during World War II.

George W. Bush found the White House much as his father had—never in better shape. Some small alterations were made in the private quarters, as usual, and, as is customary, the Oval Office—which got a new permanent carpet—and the Cabinet Room were redecorated; the former to make a statement about the President's personal interests and tastes, and the latter to send a message about his men he regards as his role models.

After the terrorist attacks on the World Trade Center and the Pentagon, the "People's House" was closed to the public, as it had been during World War I. It was eventually reopened then, and will be again one day.

Although President Bill Clinton was better known as a jogger, he was also an avid golfer, and practiced his shots on the White House putting green.

President George W. Bush made few changes to the White House, but he and First Lady, Laura, oversaw the design and installation of a new rug in the Oval Office.

The Dog House

President Bush's dogs, Barney and Spot, sometimes travel with him. But they're always glad to get home.

President Lyndon Johnson's beagles, Him and Her, were a favorite photo opportunity for the White House press corps.

A cat named Socks was the only White House pet during the early part of the Clinton administration.

All of the early presidents had horses, and usually cows as well, on the White House grounds. The last presidential cow was William Howard Taft's Pauline, who went to her reward in the early years of the twentieth century. Horses were still living there in the Kennedy administration.

More recent presidents have considered it important to have a dog or two around the place to show their common touch, a quality Americans pride above almost everything else in their chief executives.

George W. Bush has two dogs, an English Springer Spaniel named Spot, and a Scottish Terrier whose name is Barney. His wife, Laura, has a black cat she calls India, and the President's mother even wrote a book about her dog, Millie.

Lyndon B. Johnson had a pair of hounds that he loved to pick up by the ears to shock the press corps. Their names were Him and Her. And possibly the most famous White House dog of them all was FDR's black Scottish Terrier, Falla. It was said that he took Falla with him to the Yalta Conference during World War II, and somehow the dog missed the boat when it was

time to go home, so the President allegedly sent a Navy ship to go back and pick him up.

When Bill Clinton acquired his Labrador retriever, Buddy, it didn't get along with the family cat, Socks. Nobody could stop the fights and Socks, who was there first, was shipped off to live elsewhere. As was the case with most presidential pets, Buddy had the run of the White House, but he was never seen in the Cabinet Room. On the other hand, Warren G. Harding's Airedale, Laddie Boy, had a chair reserved for him there.

But not every presidential pet was a cat or a dog. Thomas Jefferson was especially fond of his pet mockingbird, and he had a distant relationship with a pair of grizzly bear cubs that roamed the White House grounds.

Abraham Lincoln kept a pair of goats in the White House, and Benjamin Harrison had one, too. Harrison also bought several ferrets, although not as pets; the White House had

The presidential cat had to be exiled when a dog named Buddy came to White House. They fought like, well, cats and dogs.

always been plagued with rats, and he hoped they would eliminate the problem. They didn't.

Grover Cleveland had a poodle, but he also had several canaries, a monkey, and a very large family of rabbits. At his home away from the White House, the menagerie included foxes and white rats. There are no reports that he or his wife ever befriended the black ones down in the basement.

As might be expected, the Theodore Roosevelts filled the place with wildlife, some of it still alive. Young Alice had her pet garter snake, of course, but the inventory extended to a pony, a kangaroo rat, a macaw, and a parrot. It isn't known whether the parrot ever had anything to say, but William McKinley had one that could whistle *Yankee Doodle*.

Harry Truman didn't have any pets, but he was very fond of the squirrels on the White House Lawn. When President Eisenhower built a golf driving range out there, he had the animals removed to Rock Creek Park, but a citizen recaptured them and dumped them back on the grounds through the fence.

Herbert Hoover's son, Allan, had a pair of pet alligators that he kept in the bathtub upstairs. But every now and then they

managed to get loose for a little exploring of the rest of the house.

The Kennedy family took care of three dogs, Clipper, a German Shepherd, a Welsh terrier named Charlie, and Puskina, the daughter of the first dog in space that was given to JFK by Soviet Premier Nikita Khrushchev. They also had a canary and a pair of lovebirds, a kitten, some ducks, and a pair of ponies.

4 The Grand Tour

Although temporarily suspended in the wake of terrorist attacks in 2001, for generations, the White House public tour has been number one on the list of things to do when Americans make a pilgrimage to Washington. It routinely attracted more than 8,000 people a day, and hundreds more were turned away for lack of available tickets. The public rooms they visited, and surely will again, include those on the following pages.

RIGHT

White House tours were temporarily suspended on November 29, 2001. But the gates will open again some day soon.

FAR RIGHT

When White House tours are available, more than 8,000 people show up for them every day, but few of them seem to bother to dress for the occasion.

White House

All White House tours have been suspended until further notice.

White House Visitor Center
15th at E Street

THE VERMEIL ROOM

When she was First Lady, Mamie Eisenhower frequently entertained her close friend, Margaret Thompson Biddle, at the White House. When she died in 1956, Mrs. Biddle bequeathed a collection of some 1,575 pieces of gilded silver, known as vermeil, to the White House Collection. When it arrived in 1958, special cabinets were built in this ground-floor room, which had served as a billiard room during the Wilson administration.

Mrs. Biddle, who had inherited an impressive Montana mining fortune, lived for most of her life in Paris, and entertained lavishly there. Her guest list frequently included the Eisenhowers, during Ike's time as Commander of NATO. Over the years, she collected silver gilt, which made her parties that much more memorable.

Most of the pieces are European, including vases, flatware, tureens, candelabra, wine coolers, baskets, and trays crafted by the best French and English silversmiths of the eighteenth and nineteenth centuries. There are some American pieces in the collection, as well, including Gorham dinner plates and Tiffany goblets.

The room itself, which is often called the Gold Room, has early nineteenth-century green silk draperies, and a pale green Turkish rug. The top of the circular mahogany Empire-style table in the center of the room is veneered in twelve pie-shaped sections, each containing a brass star. The huge cut glass chandelier above it was made in England in the late eighteenth century, about a dozen years after the Revolutionary War.

There is a Duncan Phyfe sofa with scrolled ends along the south wall, and two pairs of American Empire card tables along the east and west walls.

THE LIBRARY

When First Lady Jacqueline Kennedy embarked on her ambitious program of redecorating the White House in 1961, she enlisted the help of the Fine Arts Commission, and a committee of historians, decorators, and other authorities.

Among them was the American Institute of Interior Designers, which volunteered to refurbish the ground floor Library. A committee was established under the direction of James T. Babb, the librarian at Yale University's Beinecke Library, to assemble a collection of significant books by important American authors. The AID, meanwhile, went to work creating a setting for them.

Among the things they tracked down were a desk and a gilded chandelier, among other pieces, from the home of the American author, James Fenimore Cooper. They also located a neoclassical mantel from a house in Salem, Massachusetts. It is graced by a pair of silver Argand lamps that had been a gift from the Marquis de Lafayette to General Henry Knox, Washington's Secretary of War. The lamps, which give off a stronger light than candles with

BELOW

First Lady Rosalynn Carter said she was "determined to be taken seriously," and soon after her husband's inauguration, she took a goodwill tour of South America as his representative.

less soot, were the preferred lighting used by Presidents Washington, Jefferson, and Madison.

The room itself was a laundry room until Theodore Roosevelt's 1902 renovation, which converted it into a "Gentleman's Ante-Room."

THE CHINA ROOM

Over the years, it had been customary for incoming First Families to buy new china and sell off what had been left for them to use. It wasn't until Caroline Harrison, the wife of President Benjamin Harrison, arrived on the scene that the custom began to change.

ABOVE

Jacqueline Kennedy worked closely with members of the American Institute of Interior Design to refurbish the White House Library in the style of the eighteenth century.

LEFT

Before the 1962 redecoration, the Library was a rather ordinary room by any standards. Originally a laundry room, it had been designated a "Gentlemen's Ante-Room" after the building's 1902 renovation.

ABOVE

As First Lady, Mamie Eisenhower greatly expanded the White House china collection with items from families of former presidents.

ABOVE RIGHT

This plate features the Great Seal of the United States. The Presidential Seal didn't appear on state china until the Wilson administration.

RIGHT

Mrs. Benjamin Harrison proposed an expansion of the White House, and though the Senate approved her plan, the House never voted on it.

An art student with a special interest in china, she had the building thoroughly cleaned from top to bottom, and any china that was discovered in nooks and crannies, she had repaired and stored in a china closet. It was the beginning of the collection that is now in the China Room.

Established by Edith Wilson in 1917 as the "Presidential Collection Room," this is the only room in the house that reflects the taste of America's presidents and their wives. The pieces that Caroline Harrison had squirreled away were augmented by donations from presidential families. Almost every past president is represented in the collection, which is arranged chronologically.

The portrait of Mrs. Calvin Coolidge, which sets the red color standard for the room, was painted by Howard Chandler Christie, one of the most prolific creators of pin-up art in the 1920s. According to one story, he went to Washington to do a portrait of the president, but when the man was too busy to sit for him, he painted Grace instead.

THE DIPLOMATIC RECEPTION ROOM

In 1960, not long before they moved out of the White House, President and Mrs. Eisenhower accepted a gift of furnishings for the Diplomatic Reception Room from the National Society of Interior Designers. It was the first time that museum-quality pieces were introduced to the White House, beginning a trend that still continues today.

The Society assembled the collection through donations from private collectors and from leading dealers. All of the pieces represent the

best that American furniture-makers produced in the early nineteenth century, the period when the house itself was built.

The room is the formal entrance to the White House from the South Grounds and is the entrance the First Family generally uses, as well as the place where ambassadors arrive to present their credentials to the president. In an earlier time, it was the furnace room, which may explain why President Franklin D. Roosevelt used it as the setting for his famous "fireside chats."

The National Society of Interior Designers reentered the picture during the Kennedy administration, when it donated the historic French wallpaper that had been removed from a house in Maryland. The paper, printed from woodblocks, is called "Views From America," showing idyllic scenes of places Europeans found fascinating back in 1834. The scenes are of New York and Boston harbors, Niagara Falls, Natural Bridge, and West Point. It is entirely appropriate for a room designated for receiving foreign diplomats.

ABOVE

After the White House was rebuilt, President Truman led Walter Cronkite on a tour that was broadcast live on television. It began in the Diplomatic Reception Room.

King Hussein of Jordan was given a presidential tour of the building by Bill Clinton in 1995. VIP guests often get such tours on their first White House visits.

THE MAP ROOM

President Franklin D. Roosevelt spent a lot of time in this room, which he used as a situation room to keep track of the events of World War II. President Nixon had it converted into a sitting room, and it was furnished in the late eighteenth-century Chippendale style. Most of the pieces were made in Philadelphia and New York in the early 1770s.

The sandstone mantel was cut from stone that had been used in the house's foundation and was replaced during the massive rebuilding during the Truman administration. The last situation map, prepared in the room for President Roosevelt in 1943, hangs over it. The map on the east wall is an engraving made from a chart created by colonial surveyors, Joshua Fry and Thomas Jefferson's father, Peter Jefferson. Behind it is a case of world maps given to the White House by the National Geographic Society.

THE EAST ROOM

The largest room in the White House, the East Room was designed to be the major reception room. When architect James Hoban rebuilt the house in 1818 after fire destroyed it four years earlier, he added a gilded plaster frieze that hadn't been in the original room. President Monroe ordered a suite of twenty-four mahogany chairs and four matching sofas for the room. But the room itself stood unpainted and empty, its doors locked, for the next ten years. It was mostly used for storage, although once in awhile it was used for dancing. The

When Theodore Roosevelt and his family arrived at the White House, they found the East Room decked with flags for a military reception.

problem, as usual, was money. The President's enemies in Congress refused to pay for finishing the East Room after sending a message that "people can dance as well, or even better, in an empty room, than in one crowded with furniture." By the time money was forthcoming, John Quincy Adams had taken charge and he spent it on general repairs.

Andrew Jackson finally squeezed out the necessary funds, and went all out to convert the room into a showplace. The inventory included lemon-colored, cloth-edged wallpaper, light blue curtains and yellow draperies topped by cornices with gilded eagles, mahogany furniture, heavy mirrors, and almost 500 yards of carpeting. The feature that caused the most impressive comments was the chandeliers. Nobody had ever seen any quite as fine. They, incidentally, were replaced by even grander versions five years later, and the originals were moved to the dining rooms. The replacements were themselves replaced in 1873.

Even Jackson's detractors had to admit that his East Room, "by far excels any in the country." But over the years, a lot of use and a lot of neglect had rendered it a bit dowdy—President Lincoln had even used it as a

temporary barracks for Union soldiers during the Civil War. It was repainted and put back into repair during the Andrew Johnson years, and then completely redone in 1902, when President Theodore Roosevelt hired the architectural firm of McKim, Mead & White to transform it into a Classical style.

As if to repeat the congressional comment that dancing is more easily accomplished in a room without furniture, this room, which is used for balls and parties, receptions, and even funerals, is virtually unfurnished. The Steinway grand piano in the center, supported by gilt American eagles, is about all there is except for about two-dozen chairs. The portrait of George Washington by Gilbert Stuart that hangs in the East Room is the same one that Dolley Madison saved from the 1814 fire.

LEFT

Harry Truman, a pretty good piano player, was invited back to the White House to play for President Kennedy and his official family, including Vice President Lyndon Johnson.

BELOW

The East Room as it looked in 1948. It is the scene of more historic events than any other room in the White House, and is often used for balls and receptions.

When Raisa Gorbachev, First Lady of the Soviet Union, visited the White House, America's First Lady, Nancy Reagan, led her on a tour that included the Green Room, which Thomas Jefferson had used as a dining room.

The Blue Room has been restored to what it looked like during James Monroe's presidency. The walls are hung in cream-striped satin below a blue-draped valance trimmed with a tasseled border.

THE GREEN ROOM

This was used as a spare bedroom when John and Abigail Adams lived in the house, but Thomas Jefferson converted it to a dining room. He had the floor covered with green canvas, and the room has been one shade or another of green ever since.

The Green Room was usually used as a parlor for the relaxation of presidential families, and just about all of them furnished it to reflect their personal taste until Theodore Roosevelt's makeover set a historical style by introducing antique reproductions. Later, the Coolidges added genuine antiques, and the room became a showplace for the Federal style, popular in America in the early years of the nineteenth century.

THE BLUE ROOM

An elliptical room, mirroring the Diplomatic Reception Room beneath it and the Yellow Oval Room above, the Blue Room has nearly always been used as a reception room.

It is furnished in the French Empire style, established when President Monroe

The Red Room is furnished in the American Empire style popular in the early nineteenth century. It was refurbished in 2000, using American-made fabrics for wall coverings and upholstery. The chandelier, made in 1805, is carved and gilded wood.

redecorated it. Many of the pieces he had shipped here from France are still in the room. The marble-topped table in the center and the chandelier above it were among Madison's contributions.

When Martin Van Buren had the room redecorated in 1837, he didn't alter the style, but he did change the color. He chose blue, and blue it still is. A restoration in the 1990s kept to the color scheme, with the drapery fabric and upholstery a close match to what Van Buren apparently had in mind. But this is clearly Madison's room. When the chairs were reupholstered, the gold medallions in the shape of eagles on the backs of the chairs were copied from a portrait of Madison that included one of them.

THE RED ROOM

The Red Room was refurbished in 2000, following the rich American Empire style established in 1962 during the Kennedy restoration. All of the fabrics in the room are American-made, based on French Empire Designs. The walls are covered in red satin with gold borders and the furniture is covered in matching silk.

The Red Room was created as the "President's Antechamber," placed next to the Cabinet Room. It was given a new use during the Madison administration when it was converted into the "Yellow Drawing Room," the scene of Dolley Madison's weekly receptions. In later administrations it was used as a parlor, and many presidents have also used it for intimate dinner parties.

The State Dining Room can seat 140 guests. It was expanded to its present size during the 1902 renovation. It wasn't officially called the State Dining Room until the Jackson administration, although it was used for formal dinners before then.

Before its expansion, the State Dining Room was cluttered with heavy Victorian detail popular back in the late 1850s.

THE ENTRANCE HALL AND THE CROSS HALL

Of all the alterations that have been made to the White House, these two halls are still as architect James Hoban envisioned them.

Of course, that isn't to say they haven't been changed a bit. In the original plan, there were two wide stairways leading up to the second floor, but one of them was eliminated for the expansion of the State Dining Room. The other was enlarged at the same time, and then in a later renovation it was moved to open directly into the Entrance Hall.

The resulting Grand Stairway has become the centerpiece of many White House ceremonials. On state occasions, the president greets his special guests upstairs in the Yellow

Oval Room, and then they slowly walk down the stairs to greet the other guests in the East Room. It is an unforgettable ritual, with Marine guards standing at attention and the Marine Band playing *Hail to The Chief*. A glittering cut-glass chandelier hanging above the first landing adds a touch of exciting elegance.

Everything in the White House is intended to impress visitors, but the impression is never quite as dramatic as at the foot of this stairway during a presidential reception.

OFF THE BEATEN PATH

Even when tours of the White House are possible, there are some rooms tourists, for obvious reasons, never get to see.

THE WEST WING

Quite the busiest part of the White House, the West Wing contains the Oval Office, the Cabinet Room, the offices of the executive staff, the press room, and the Roosevelt Room where the President meets and greets large groups.

The wing, which follows the outlines of Thomas Jefferson's terraced annexes to the White House, was constructed in 1902 during Theodore Roosevelt's administration. Prior to that the executive functions took place on the second floor, which was also where the president and his family lived. TR had a large, rambunctious family, and he was probably quite relieved to move downstairs.

ABOVE

George Bush and his wife, Barbara, hosted a diplomatic reception for Swedish officials in 1989. As always on these occasions, the President and First Lady lead their special guests down the Grand Staircase to the East Room.

You might ask, does the president always wear a suit jacket when he's at work in the Oval Office? Bill Clinton did on his first weekend there in 1993.

George W. Bush was wearing his jacket when he was photographed in the Oval Office in 2001. So the answer to that question might be another question: Does the camera lie?

THE OVAL OFFICE

Until 1909, when the first Oval Office was built, presidents usually worked in office suites in the Residence, each configuring space to suit his own work habits.

The original Oval Office was located on the south side of the West Wing, but was moved to the southeast corner, overlooking the Rose Garden, in 1932. As in the past, every president furnishes the office to suit his own taste and work patterns. Some things are never changed, though. The white marble mantelpiece from the older office is a constant, as are the Presidential Seal on the ceiling, and the flags behind the desk.

President George W. Bush has decorated the office with paintings of scenes of his native Texas by Texan artists. All of them are on loan from museums there.

The desk he works behind is called the *Resolute* desk. It was made from the oak timbers of a British ship that had been trapped in Arctic ice, and was towed out by an American whaler. The U.S. Government had the ship repaired and refitted and presented her to England's Queen Victoria as a token of friendship between the two countries. The Queen returned the favor and sent the desk to President Rutherford B. Hayes in 1880 as a memorial of "the courage and loving kindness

In March 1970 President Nixon installed a new Cabinet table, paying $4,500 out of his own money for the 22½-ft (6.9-m) long table. It had a mahogany heirloom-finished rim with a cowhide center.

which dictated the offer." It has been used by every president since then, except Presidents Johnson, Nixon, and Ford.

It had been placed in various locations around the White House, and didn't get carried into the Oval Office in 1961 for President Kennedy. It has been modified a few times. Franklin D. Roosevelt had the kneehole covered with a panel bearing the Presidential Seal, and Ronald Reagan had it raised a couple of inches to make room for his long legs.

THE CABINET ROOM

Located close to the Oval Office, this is where the president meets with his Cabinet, the National Security Council, congressional delegations, and visiting heads of state.

The huge oval table that dominates the room was a gift from President Nixon in 1970. For Cabinet meetings, the President sits at the center of the east side of it, and the Vice President sits directly across from him. The Secretary of State sits directly on the President's right, and the other Cabinet members are assigned positions around the table arranged according to the date the department was formed.

Like the Oval Office, the Cabinet Room overlooks the Rose Garden. Its decorations are licenses of former presidents and statesmen selected by the sitting president. President Bush

has chosen busts of George Washington and Benjamin Franklin, and portraits of Presidents Jefferson, Theodore Roosevelt, and Eisenhower.

THE EAST WING

Completing the Classical symmetry of the White House, the East Wing replaced a greenhouse in 1942 as a base of operations for the First Lady and her staff.

The Jacqueline Kennedy Garden outside, which was named by First Lady Bird Johnson in honor of her predecessor, serves as a reception area for the president's wife. When the weather cooperates, of course.

The Jacqueline Kennedy Garden near the East Wing was dedicated in 1965 by another First Lady, Mrs. Lyndon B. Johnson.

Afterword

On the last night of his presidency, Ronald Reagan addressed the nation from the Oval Office. The following are a few excerpts from his talk:

"Down the hall and up the stairs from this office is the part of the White House where the president and his family live. There are a few favorite windows I have up there that I like to stand and look out of early in the morning. The view is over the grounds here to the Washington Monument, and then the Mall and the Jefferson Memorial. But on mornings when the humidity is low, you can see past the Jefferson to the river, the Potomac, and the Virginia shore. Someone said that's the view Lincoln had when he saw the smoke rising from the Battle of Bull Run."

"...But now, we're entering the nineties and some things have changed. Younger parents aren't so sure that an unambivalent appreciation of America is the right thing to teach modern children. And for those who create the popular culture, well-grounded patriotism is no longer the style. Our [patriotic] spirit is back, but we haven't reinstitutionalized it. We've got to do a better job of getting across that America is freedom—freedom of speech, freedom of religion, freedom of enterprise. And freedom is special and rare. It's fragile; it needs protection."

"...So, we've got to teach history based not on what's in fashion, but what's important—why the Pilgrims came here, who Jimmy Doolittle was, and what Thirty Seconds Over Tokyo meant...If we forget what we did, we won't know who we are. I'm warning of an eradication of the American memory that could result, ultimately, in an erosion of the American spirit. Let's start with some basics: more attention to American history and a greater emphasis on civic ritual."

Acknowledgments

The publishers wish to thank the following photographers and picture libraries who have supplied photographs for this book. Photographs have been credited by page number and position on the page: (T) top, (B) bottom, (L) left, (R) right, (C) center.

Front and back jacket Chrysalis Images; 1 Archivo Iconografico, S.A./Corbis; 2 Peter Newark's Pictures; 3 Chrysalis Images; 4–5 Bettmann/Corbis; 8–9 Corbis; 10(B) Chrysalis Images; 10–11 Hulton|Archive; 12 MPI/Hulton|Archive; 13(T) Corbis; 14 Hulton|Archive; 15(T) Architects of the Capitol; 15(B) Corbis; 16 Corbis; 17(B) Bettmann/Corbis; 18(T) Architects of the Capitol; 18(B) Corbis; 19 Peter Newark's Pictures; 20 Corbis; 21(T) USPS; 21(B) Corbis; 22(T) Hulton|Archive; 22(B) Chrysalis Images; 24 Corbis; 25(T) Corbis; 25(B) Smithsonian Institution; 26(B) Tom Nebbia/Corbis; 26–27 Chrysalis Images; 28(T) Chrysalis Images; 28(B) Bettmann/Corbis; 29(T) Chrysalis Images; 29(B) Chrysalis Images; 30 MPI/Hulton|Archive; 32 Bettmann/Corbis; 33(T) Chrysalis Images; 33(B) Chrysalis Images; 34(T) MPI/Hulton|Archive; 34(B) Bequest of Mrs. Benjamin Ogle Taylor: Collection of the Corcoran Gallery of Art/Corbis; 36(T) Chrysalis Images; 36(B) Hulton|Archive; 38(T) Chrysalis Images; 38(B) Corbis; 39 MPI/Hulton|Archive; 40(T) Bettmann/Corbis; 40(B) Chrysalis Images; 42(T) Chrysalis Images; 42(B) Bettmann/Corbis; 43(T) Chrysalis Images; 43(B) Bettmann/Corbis; 44(T) Three Lions/Hulton|Archive; 44(B) Hulton; 45(T) Chrysalis Images; 45(B) Chrysalis Images; 46(L) Chrysalis Images; 46(R) Bettmann/Corbis; 48(T) Stock Montage/Archive Photos; 48(B) Corbis; 49(T) Chrysalis Images; 49(B) Corbis; 50(T) Chrysalis Images; 50(B) Stock Montage/Archive Photos; 52(T) Chrysalis Images; 52(B) Bettmann/Corbis; 53(T) Chrysalis Images; 53(B) Hulton|Archive; 54(L) Chrysalis Images; 54(R) Museum of the City of New York/Archive Photos; 55(T) Bettmann/Corbis; 55(B) Hulton|Archive; 56(B) Corbis; 56–57 Chrysalis Images; 58 Library of Congress/Hulton|Archive; 59(T) Corbis; 59(B) Archive Photos; 60(T) Corbis; 61(T) Library of Congress/Hulton|Archive; 61(B) Bettmann/Corbis; 62(T) Chrysalis Images; 62(B) Bettmann/Corbis; 64(T) Corbis; 64(B) Corbis; 65(T) Chrysalis Images; 65(B) Corbis; 66(T) Bettmann/Corbis; 66(B) Chrysalis Images; 68(B) Bettmann/Corbis; 69(T) Bettmann/Corbis; 69(B) Bettmann/Corbis; 70(T) Bettmann/Corbis; 70(B) Chrysalis Images; 72(L) Chrysalis Images; 72(R) Bettmann/Corbis; 73(T) Bettmann/Corbis; 73(C) Bettmann/Corbis; 73(B) Corbis; 74(T) Corbis; 74(B) Bettmann/Corbis; 75(T) Matthew Mendelsohn/Corbis; 75(B) Reuters/Larry Downing; 76(T) Reuters/Win McNamee; 76(C) Bettmann/Corbis; 76(BL) Larry Downing/Corbis Sygma; 76(BR) Reuters/Win McNamee; 77(T) Bettmann/Corbis; 77(B) John F. Kennedy Library/Hulton|Archive; 78(B) Reuters/Larry Downing; 78–79 Bettmann/Corbis; 80 Bettmann/Corbis; 81(T) Bettmann/Corbis; 81(B) Corbis; 82(TL) Bettmann/Corbis; 82(B) Corbis; 83 Bettmann/Corbis; 84(T) Kinney/CNP/Corbis Sygma; 84(B) Underwood & Underwood/Corbis; 85(T) Bettmann/Corbis; 85(B) Bettmann/Corbis; 86(T) Bettmann/Corbis; 86(B) Bettmann/Corbis; 87 Bettmann/Corbis; 88(T) Bettmann/Corbis; 88(B) Corbis; 89 Bettmann/Corbis; 90(T) Win McNamee/Corbis; 90(C) Reuters/Win McNamee; 91(T) Bettmann/Corbis; 91(B) Bettmann/Corbis; 92–93 Ronald Reagan Library/Archive Photos; 94–95 Reuters/HO/Paul Morse